FAULT DETECTABILITY IN DWDM

Books of Related Interest from the IEEE Press

INTRODUCTION TO DWDM TECHNOLOGY: Data in a Rainbow
Stamatios V. Kartalopoulos
2000   Hardcover   274 pp   IEEE Order No. PC5831   ISBN 0-7803-5399-4

UNDERSTANDING SONET/SDH AND ATM: Communications Networks for the Next Millennium
Stamatios V. Kartalopoulos
A volume in the IEEE Press Understanding Science & Technology Series
1999   Softcover   288 pp   IEEE Order No. PP5399   ISBN 0-7803-4745-5

FAULT DETECTABILITY IN DWDM

Toward Higher Signal Quality
& System Reliability

Stamatios V. Kartalopoulos
Lucent Technologies, Inc.
Bell Labs Innovations
Holmdel, NJ

IEEE PRESS

The Institute of Electrical and Electronics Engineers, Inc., New York

This book and other books may be purchased at a discount
from the publisher when ordered in bulk quantities. Contact:

IEEE Press Marketing
Attn: Special Sales
445 Hoes Lane, P.O. Box 1331
Piscataway, NJ 08855-1331
Fax: +1 732 981 9334

For more information about IEEE Press products, visit the
IEEE Online Store & Catalog: http://www.ieee.org/store.

IEEE Order No. PC5886

Library of Congress Cataloging-in-Publication Data

Kartalopoulos, Stamatios V.
    Fault detectability in DWDM: toward higher signal quality & system reliability /
Stamatios V. Kartalopoulos.
        p. cm.
    Includes bibliographical references and index.
    ISBN 978-0-7803-6044-0
    1. Optical communications.   2. Multiplexing.   3. Signal processing—Digital
techniques.   4. Fault location (Engineering)   I. Title.
    TK5103.59.K34   2001
    621.382′7—dc21   00-053533

To my parents for my first breath in life,
To my first teacher for her inspiration,
To my wife, Anita, for her love and encouragement,
To my children Vasilis (William) and Stephanie
for the many joys they have brought me,
And to all those who have enriched my life.

CONTENTS

PREFACE

For more than 2500 years, light has been used in communications. In those days, light towers were used to send quickly a brief encoded message from point A to point B and across the land, such as "the enemy is approaching" or "festivities will start next month."

Communicating with light in open space, although a seemingly simple operation, had its own problems. For example, when a robust code was used so that the enemy could not easily decode the message, many factors had to be considered. The light should be intense enough so that it could be seen from a distant tower. The tower should be strategically positioned and be tall enough so that trees and low hills could not obstruct the line of sight. The atmosphere should be clear so that heavy rain or fog could not absorb the optical signal. The towers should be adequately equipped and staffed. A synchronization mechanism should exist so that the receiving tower would know when a message was about to be transmitted. A protocol should be followed so that when the received message was not understood, a request to retransmit could be made. And, of course, there were many maintenance functions that are not too difficult to imagine. As problematic as it was, this method of optical communication lasted until a couple of centuries ago.

Throughout history many scientists made significant contributions in the optical domain. The reflectivity and refractivity of light were studied, and in ancient times the paraboloid reflector was studied and invented. Although in antiquity glass was not as clear as it is today, it generated a lucrative industry primarily in the making of jewelry and of perfume vessels and in other more "exotic" applications of refracting light to perhaps form the first lens systems. Thus, glass evolved and in modern times it is a ubiquitous material. It would be very difficult today to envision life without glass. Only in the far future might we envision ourselves without it, when high-technology transparent plastics, better and more cost-efficient than glass, might replace it.

Today, glass is used in a myriad of ways, including optical communication lines. Glass-based fiber is wrapped around the globe like a ball of yarn connecting all continents and transmitting enormous amounts of data at the speed of light. Currently, a single fiber can transmit the contents of hundreds of thousands of volumes of data within a second.

Since glass and optical components provide key functionality in communications, there are visions of an all-optical network able to carry unprecedented amounts of information over many hundreds of thousands of kilometers without converting the optical signal into electronic and back to optical. The only electrical-to-optical conversion, and vice versa, will be at the end terminals, at the source and at the sink of the signal, respectively.

ABOUT THIS BOOK

My interest in the field of optical communication has culminated in two books, *Introduction to DWDM Technology: Data in a Rainbow* (IEEE Press, 2000) and *Understanding SONET/SDH and ATM: Communications Networks for the Next Millenium* (IEEE Press, 1999). Recently, I have been working on the evaluation of faults and degradations of optical components in multiwavelength systems and networks, on fault detectability and localization, and also on the necessary remedial actions. Degradations and faults of optical components is an integral part of system and network design that cannot be overlooked. For example, degradations and faults affect the quality of the optical signal and thus the optical signal-to-noise ratio, the optical bit error rate, and the fiber span without amplification. In addition, they affect the selection of the forward error correction (FEC) code, the receiver design, fail-safe mechanisms, monitoring strategies and remedial actions, and in general fault management, as well as the system and network robustness. At the ultrahigh bit rates and aggregate bandwidth used today, such degradations and faults should be identified as soon as they happen and remedied.

My personal notes and several documents that I have published provided the source material for this book. In many respects, this book is the continuation of *Introduction to DWDM Technology: Data in a Rainbow,* which describes the properties of light, its interaction with matter, and how optical components work in optical communications, such as filters, multiplexers, optical switches, and many others. This book provides only a brief overview of key principles and optical components and focuses on the understanding of optical fault and degradation mechanisms (detection, localization, and remedial action) that affect the optical signal and the operation of the DWDM system and perhaps of the network. The understanding of optical faults and degradations is important in the architectural design of optical systems and networks, in the design of complex optical components, in fault management of dense wavelength division multiplexing (DWDM) systems and networks, and in the development of standards. DWDM technology is still evolving, and as such, the reader interested in the details of DWDM is strongly recommended to consult the most current updated standards. I wish you happy and easy reading.

Stamatios V. Kartalopoulos, Ph.D.
Lucent Technologies, Inc.
Bell Labs Innovations

ACKNOWLEDGMENTS

Throughout time, few achievements of note have been the product of individual effort. Instead, they have been accomplished through the efforts of many. Similarly, the fruition of this book would be impossible without the cooperation, diligence, understanding, and encouragement of a number of people. First, I would like to extend my thanks and appreciation to my wife, Anita, for her patience and encouragement. I would also like to extend my thanks to my colleagues, for creating an environment that fosters learning, collaboration, and encouragement. In particular, I would like to thank Sjoerd Last and Harvey Epstein for stimulating discussion on this subject as well as the anonymous reviewers for their comments and constructive criticism and to the IEEE Press staff for their enthusiasm, suggestions, creativity, and project management. Finally, I am grateful to all those who diligently worked on all execution phases of this production.

Stamatios V. Kartalopoulos, Ph.D.
Lucent Technologies, Inc.
Bell Labs Innovations

INTRODUCTION

Since early history, the fascination with light has sparked the curiosity and imagination of mankind. It was so difficult to explain its origin that many ancient cultures resorted to myths; according to one, Prometheus brought fire to mankind and Apollo was the son of Light (Sun); and others attributed divine properties to crystals with irridescent properties. Most ancient theologies linked light with the divine, and many modern ones still do.

Many scientists have attempted to provide a scientific interpretation of the origin of light; they linked light with atomic energy levels. According to this model, light is the result of electrons or energy states when they "jump" from a higher state to a lower one. Then, energy is emitted in the form of an electromagnetic wave, which may be in the visible or invisible spectrum. However, this electromagnetic energy is special; the wave is self-propelled and propagates even in "emptiness," a concept that has many believers and also many skeptics. In addition to being a wave, light also exhibits particle properties. For instance, when light falls on a specially prepared wheel, it makes the wheel spin (*Compton's* experiment). However, the notion of two natures coexisting in light is still difficult to grasp, even though Einstein has linked energy with mass ($E = mc^2$). Despite this, the fact remains that science has demystified the "divinity" of crystals, and semiconductor devices (the laser) generate a photonic beam at command. This beam is so powerful and so "narrow" that it can be applied in a wide range of applications—in communications, in land surveys, and in surgical operations, to mention a few.

Optical waves extend over a wide spectrum of frequencies (or wavelengths). However, this spectrum is not entirely visible to the human eye. What we call *visible light* is in a narrow range of wavelengths, from 0.7 μm (700 nm) to 0.4 μm (400 nm), from the deep red to the dark violet-blue; this is so because of the response range of the human retinal receptors (the cones and the rods). Had we asked a cat or an owl how things appear through their own eyes, we would certainly get a different answer. The optical spectrum used in high-speed fiber communications is beyond the visible spectrum; it is in the range of 1200–1700 nm for reasons dictated by the optical medium and the components.

In optical communications, bit rates of up to 40 Gbps are currently used in a single-mode fiber, and bit rates higher than that have been demonstrated. At 40 Gbps, half a million simultaneous telephone conversations can be supported. *Dense wavelength-division multiplexing* (DWDM) technology increases the aggregate bandwidth to terabits per second. DWDM systems with more than a hundred wavelengths in the same fiber are here, and DWDM technologies with 206 wavelengths or more have been experimentally demonstrated. An 80-wavelength DWDM system at 40 Gbps per wavelength has an aggregate bandwidth of 3200 Gbps, a bandwidth that can transport in a single fiber the contents of many thousand volumes of an encyclopedia in a second. Therefore, the optical signal that carries such vast amounts of information should be safeguarded to maintain an acceptable quality level throughout its complete traveled path, through fibers and optical components.

However, one should not lose sight of the fact that:

- Light interacts with matter as well as with itself.

- The parameters of many optical components depend on temperature, stress, time (aging), and in some cases electrical or magnetic fields.

- Optical components degrade or fail and these degradation or failures are not observed in a traditional manner, as are their electronic counterparts.

All these degradations and failures may have a direct effect on the quality of the signal and/or the availability of the system/network and, most importantly, the availability of the service provided to the end user. Therefore, imminent degradations and faults must be promptly identified and either remedied or bypassed, else a tremendous amount of data may be lost or not delivered, considering the amount of data that bandwidths at the terabits-per-second level carry. That is, in a multifiber and multiwavelength network, the availability of terabits-per-second bandwidth may not be as critical as it may be the inability to transport this bandwidth due to faults and degradations. Consequently, "photonic" degradations and failures in DWDM systems and networks should be thoroughly understood to assist in an efficient fault detection, localization, restoration, and avoidance strategy that assures the quality of signal and a reliable communications network.

IN THIS BOOK

The objective of this book is to enhance the understanding of degradation and failure mechanisms of optical components and to assist in drafting fault detection guidelines that could be used to design a more robust multiwavelength optical system and network. A thorough overview of optical components can be found in the book, *Introduction to DWDM Technology: Data in a Rainbow,* (IEEE Press, 2000) by the same author, as well as in other publications.

This book is organized into six chapters, and progressively introduces the subject of photonic faults and degradations. Chapter 1 reviews the properties of light and optical communications; Chapter 2 reviews the optical components; Chapter 3 describes the parameters that affect the quality of the DWDM optical signal; Chapter 4 describes the faults affecting the optical DWDM signal; Chapter 5 provides a correlation of faults; and Chapter 6 gives a description of fault management aspects and identifies current issues in DWDM.

STANDARDS

Optical transmission is specified in detail in several documents published by international standards bodies. These documents are official and voluminous. This relatively brief book can only be considered a high-level tutorial that explains the workings of DWDM technology and the potential failure mechanisms. Consequently, it is strongly recommended that system designers consult these standards for details. The key international standards bodies in DWDM optical communications are as follows:

- **ITU-T** and **ITU-R:** International Telecommunications Union—Telecommunications Standardization Sector and International Telecommunications Union—Radiocommunications Sector, respectively. ITU has published several documents identified by "ITU-T Recommendation G.nnn," where nnn is a number that refers to a specific aspect of the system. Example: ITU-T Recommendation G.774.01 describes the Synchronous Digital Hierarchy (SDH) Performance Monitoring for the Network Element.

- **Telcordia Technologies, Inc.** (formerly **Bellcore**) is a U.S.-based organization that has contributed to standards and has also published technical recommendations.

- **Other known standards bodies:** American National Standards Institute (ANSI); Association Francaise de Normalisation (AFNOR); ATM-Forum; British Standards Institution (BSI); Consultative Committee International Telegraph and Telephone (CCITT), a former name of ITU; Deutsches Institut fuer Normung EV (DIN); European Association for Standardizing Information and Communication Systems (ECMA); Electronics Industry Association/Telecommunications Industry Association (EIA/TIA); European Telecommunications Standardization Institute (ETSI); Frame-Relay Forum (FRF); Institute of Electrical and Electronics Engineers (IEEE); Internet

Engineering Task Force (IETF); Motion Picture Experts Group (MPEG); International Standards Organization (ISO); Telecommunications Information Networking Architecture (TINA) consortium; Comit Europ en de Normalisation Electrotechnique (CENELEC); Personal Computer Memory Card International Association (PCMCIA); World Wide Web Consortium (W3C); and others.

CHAPTER 1

PROPERTIES OF LIGHT AND MATTER

1.1 INTRODUCTION

Fiber has been the transmission medium of choice for several years. Its use has been in long-haul applications, in metropolitan area networks (MAN), in inner city and inner campus, as well as accessing the last or first mile, such as fiber to the curb (FTTC) and fiber to the home (FTTH), whereas fiber from computer to computer is already reality.

New optical systems and networks assure that the transmission medium has a scalable transportable bandwidth capacity and that the network is scalable and flexible to pass different types of traffic at increasing capacity. Scalability is achieved by installing more fiber (or activating dark fiber), by increasing the bit rate (from 2.5 to 10 Gbps and to 40 Gbps and beyond), and by increasing the number of wavelengths per fiber [dense wavelength-division multiplexing (DWDM)]. Clearly, this implies that switching nodes in the network are able to receive scalable bandwidths, different types of traffic, and that they too have a scalable switching capacity.

As different network strategies are considered to cope with the explosive bandwidth demand, the quality of the optical signal must be maintained at a level that assures reliable and error-free (or acceptable error rate) transmission and that the availability of service must be warrantied with miniscule downtime. To achieve this, one has to first comprehend the properties of light, how light interacts with matter and with itself, and how it propagates in the fiber. In addition, one must understand how various optical components work, their degradation and failure mechanisms, how they affect the quality of the optical signal, and how we can predict or locate faults and initiate consequent remedial actions. In this chapter we examine the properties of light and how it interacts with optical materials.

1.2 NATURE OF LIGHT

Light is electromagnetic radiation that possesses two natures, a wave nature and a particle nature.

1.2.1 Wave Nature of Light

Like radio waves and X-rays, light is also electromagnetic radiation subject to reflection, refraction, diffraction, interference, polarization, fading, loss, and so on.

Light, as a wave, is characterized by frequency (and wavelength) with phase and propagation speed. The unit for frequency is cycles per second, or hertz, and the unit for wavelength is the nanometer (nm) or micrometer (μm). Another unit that occasionally is encountered is the angstrom; $1\ \text{Å} = 10^{-10}$ meters.

Light of a single frequency is termed *monochromatic,* or single color. To simplify the mathematical description of light and avoid spherical equations, we consider that the electromagnetic waves are planar. Then, monochromatic light is described by Maxwell's electromagnetic plane-wave equations: '

$$\nabla^2 \mathbf{E} = \frac{1}{c^2}\frac{\partial^2 \mathbf{E}}{\partial t^2}, \quad \nabla^2 \mathbf{H} = \frac{1}{c^2}\frac{\partial^2 \mathbf{H}}{\partial t^2}, \quad \nabla \mathbf{D} = \rho, \quad \nabla \mathbf{B} = 0$$

where ∇ is the Laplacian operator; c is a constant (the maximum speed of the wave in free space, $c = 2.99792458 \times 10^5$ km/s, or ~30 cm/ns); $\mathbf{E}$ and $\mathbf{H}$ are the electric and magnetic fields, respectively; $\mathbf{D}$ is the electric displacement vector; $\mathbf{B}$ is the magnetic induction vector; and ρ is the charge density. In practice, it is impossible to produce pure monochromatic light (i.e., a single wavelength), and this creates a number of issues that we will address later on. For theoretical analysis, however, we may consider monochromatic light.

The four field vector relations are connected with the relations

$$\mathbf{D} = \epsilon_0 \mathbf{E} + \mathbf{P} \quad \text{and} \quad \mathbf{B} = \mu_0 \mathbf{H} + \mathbf{M}$$

where ϵ_0 is the dielectric permittivity and μ_0 is the permeability, both constants of the vacuum, $\mathbf{P}$ is the electric polarization, and $\mathbf{M}$ is the magnetic polarization of the wave.

When a wave propagates through a linear medium (e.g., noncrystalline), the electric polarization is

$$\mathbf{P} = \epsilon_0 \chi \mathbf{E}$$

where χ is the electric susceptibility of the medium (in nonlinear medium this is expressed as a tensor). It turns out that the dielectric constant ϵ of the material is connected with the above medium constants by $\epsilon = \epsilon_0(1 + \chi)$.

The monochromatic plane wave has a velocity $\mathbf{v}$ in a medium that is expressed by

$$\mathbf{v} = \frac{\omega}{k} = \frac{1}{\sqrt{\mu_0 \epsilon_0}}$$

where k is a constant.

In vacuum it has a maximum constant speed c (since μ_0 and ϵ_0 are constants)

$$c = \frac{\omega}{k} = \frac{1}{\sqrt{\mu_0 \epsilon_0}}$$

From the previous relationships we establish that there are indeed dependencies between speed of light and wavelength, between speed of light and dielectric constant, and between frequency of light and dielectric constant.

1.2.2 Particle Nature of Light

The smallest quantity of monochromatic light, known as a *photon,* is described by the energy (*E*) equation:

$$E = h\nu$$

where *h* is Planck's constant, equal to $6.6260755 \times 10^{-34}$ J-s and ν is the frequency of light.

Light (from an incandescent lightbulb) consists of a continuum of wavelengths that span the entire optical spectrum from deep red (700 nm) to deep violet-blue (400 nm).

Light does not travel at the same speed in all media. In addition, each frequency travels at different speed in the same medium. In vacuum, light travels in a straight path at a constant maximum speed *c* defined by Einstein's equation (and also present in Maxwell's equations):

$$E = mc^2$$

The relationship between frequency ν, speed of light in free space c, and wavelength λ is given by

$$\nu = \frac{c}{\lambda}$$

When light travels in an optically denser (than free-space) medium (e.g., water, glass, transparent plastic), then its speed becomes slower.

1.3 REFLECTION, REFRACTION, AND DIFFRACTION

When light enters matter, its electromagnetic field reacts with the near fields of its atoms. In dense matter, light is quickly absorbed within the first few atomic layers, and since it does not emerge from it, that matter is termed *non(optically) transparent.* In contrast to this, some types of matter do not completely absorb light, letting it propagate through it and emerge from it. This is termed *optically transparent* matter. Examples of such matter are water and clear glass.

1.3.1 Reflection and Refraction: Index of Refraction

The *index of refraction* of a transparent medium (n_{med}) is defined as the ratio of the speed of light in vacuum (*c*) over the speed of light in the medium (v_{med}).

1.3.2 Diffraction

Almost any obstacle with sharp edges in the path of light, such as an aperture, a slit, or a grating (with dimensions comparable to wavelength), will cause diffraction.

According to Huygen's principle, incident waves excite secondary coherent waves at each point of the wavefront. All these waves interfere with each other and cause a diffraction pattern (i.e., each wave is diffracted at a different angle). A pure mathematical analysis of diffraction is quite involved, and it is studied by approximating the scalar Helmholz equation in which the wavefront is a spherical function. The degree of diffraction (the angle by which a ray is diffracted) depends on the wavelength. This gives rise to diffraction gratings. Although the phenomenon of diffraction is used to construct diffraction gratings, it may also be considered undesirable as causing unwanted spread of a light beam in certain optical devices and thus optical power decrease per unit area.

1.3.3 Gaussian Beams

In theory it is assumed that a beam of light has a uniform cross-sectional distribution of intensity. In reality, most beams have a radial distribution, intense in the center of the beam and reducing radially away from the center, closely matching a Gaussian distribution. Because of this intensity distribution, even if the beam is initially parallel, it does not remain so due to spatial diffraction within the beam that causes the beam to first narrow and then diverge at an angle Θ. The narrowest point in the beam is known as the *waist* of the beam (Figure 1.1).

The reality of nonuniform radial distribution introduces certain degradations that only by proper design can be compensated for.

Figure 1.1 Gaussian beam.

1.4   POLARIZATION OF LIGHT

If we examine the electrical state of matter on a microscopic level, we find out that it consists of electrical charges, the distribution of which depends on the presence or absence of external fields. If we consider that for every positive charge there is a negative, then we may think that each positive-negative pair constitues an electric dipole. The electric moment of a dipole is a function of distance and charge density. Now, if we consider a distribution of electric dipoles, then *the electric dipole moment per unit volume is termed the polarization vector* **P**.

Polarization of electromagnetic waves is, mathematically speaking, a complex subject, particularly when light propagates in a medium with different refractive indices in different directions (e.g., crystallographic axes) in it. As light propagates through a medium, it enters the fields of nearby dipoles and field interaction takes place. This interaction may affect the strength distribution of the electric and/or magnetic fields of the propagating light differently in certain directions so that the end result may be a complex field with an elliptical or a linear field distribution.

Consequently, any external or internal influences that affect the charge density distribution of the material will also affect the propagating and polarization properties of light through it.

1.4.1 Faraday Effect

Some photorefractive solid materials (e.g., α-quartz, crystallized sodium chloride) cause a rotation of the polarization plane as light travels through it. Certain liquids (cane sugar solution) and gases (camphor) also cause such rotation. This rotation is also known as the *Faraday effect*. Devices based on the Faraday effect are known as *rotators*.

In actuality, polarization rotation is explained as follows: Upon entrance in the medium, plane polarized light is decomposed into two circularly polarized waves rotating in opposite directions. Each of the two waves travels in the medium at different speed, and thus an increasing phase difference between the two is generated. Upon exiting the medium, the two waves recombine to produce a polarized wave with its polarization plane rotated by an angle, with reference to the initial polarization of the wave.

The amount of the rotation angle or *mode shift,* θ, depends on the distance traveled in the medium or on the thickness of material d (in centimeters), the magnetic field **H** (in oersteds), and a constant V, known as Verdet constant (measured in minutes per centimeter-oersted). The amount of rotation, or *mode shift,* is expressed by

$$\theta = V\mathbf{H}d$$

Clearly, any external influences that affect the constant V will also affect the amount of mode shift, θ.

1.5 PROPAGATION OF LIGHT

When light travels in a fiber, we assume that it is purely monochromatic. In general, this is a bad assumption since there is no light source that can generate a pure single optical frequency. In fact, no matter how close to perfect a monochromatic source is, there is a near-Gaussian distribution of wavelengths around a center wavelength. This is one of several reasons that optical channels in DWDM have a finite width. As a consequence, the study of optical propagation in a waveguide (optical fiber) requires the study of propagation of a group of frequencies. Two definitions are important here, the *phase velocity* and the *group velocity*.

1.5.1 Phase Velocity

A (theoretically) pure monochromatic wave (single ω or λ) that travels along the fiber axis is described by

$$\mathbf{E}(t, x) = A e^{j(\omega t - \beta x)}$$

Where A is the amplitude of the field, $\omega = 2\pi f$, and β is the propagation constant.

   Phase velocity $\mathbf{v}_\phi$ is defined as the velocity of an observer that maintains constant phase with the traveling field, that is, $\omega t - \beta x = $ const.

   Replacing the traveled distance x within time t by $x = \mathbf{v}_\phi t$, the phase velocity of the monochromatic light in the medium is

$$\mathbf{v}_\phi = \frac{\omega}{\beta}$$

1.5.2 Group Velocity

In optical communications, an optical channel does not consist of only one wavelength; that is, it is not purely monochromatic. Consequently, if we assume that an optical pulse is propagating in the fiber, we may think of it as the result of a modulated optical signal that contains frequency components within a group of optical frequencies, the optical channel. The optical modulated signal is expressed by

$$e_{AM}(t) = \mathbf{E}[1 + m\cos(\omega_1 t)]\cos(\omega_c t)$$

where $\mathbf{E}$ is the electric field, m is the modulation depth, ω_1 is the modulation frequency, ω_c is the frequency of light (or carrier frequency), and $\omega_1 \ll \omega_c$.

   However, each frequency component in the group travels in the fiber with slightly different velocity forming a traveling envelope of frequencies.

   Group velocity $\mathbf{v}_g = c/n_g$ is defined as the velocity of an observer that maintains constant phase with the group traveling envelope. The group velocity is mathematically defined as the inverse of the first derivative of the propagation constant β:

$$\mathbf{v}_g = \frac{1}{\beta'}$$

When light travels in a region of anomalous refractive index, the group and phase velocities undergo distortions (Figure 1.2).

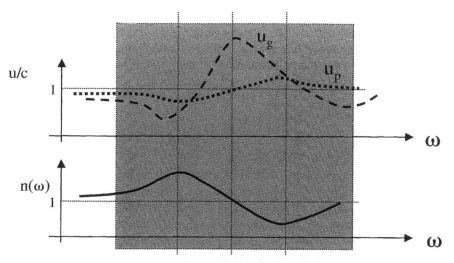

Figure 1.2 Group (u_g) and phase (u_p) velocity in a region of anomalous refractive index.

1.6 FIBER BIREFRINGENCE AND POLARIZATION

Anisotropic (crystalline) materials have a different index of refraction in specific directions within them. As such, when a beam of monochromatic unpolarized light enters such a material, it is refracted differently along the directions of different indices, and it travels along these directions at a different speed and polarization. This property of anisotropic (crystalline) materials is known as *birefringence*. Thus, an unpolarized ray that enters a birefringent material is separated into two rays, each with different polarization and different propagation constant. One ray is called *ordinary* (O) and the other *extraordinary* (E). In these two directions the refracted index is also called ordinary, n_o, and extraordinary, n_e, respectively. For example, the n_e and n_o for some birefringent crystals (measured at 1500 nm) are as follows:

Crystal	n_e	n_o
Calcite ($CaCO_3$)	1.477	1.644
Quartz (SiO_2)	1.537	1.529
Magnesium fluoride (MgF_2)	1.384	1.372

When under stress, some optically transparent isotropic materials become anisotropic as well. Stress may be exerted due to mechanical forces (pull, pressure, bend, and twist), due to thermal forces and due to strong electrical external fields. Under such conditions, the polarization and the propagation characteristics of light will be affected.

Clearly, birefringence in transmission fiber is undesirable because it alters the polarization and propagating characteristics of the optical signal.

1.7 DISPERSION

1.7.1 Modal

An optical signal propagating in a fiber may be considered as a bundle of rays. Although a serious effort is made to launch all rays parallel into the fiber, due to imperfections, the rays that comprise a narrow pulse are transmitted within a small cone. As a result, each ray in the cone (known as *mode*) travels a different path and each ray arrives at a distant point of the fiber at a different time. Thus, an initial narrow pulse will spread out due to modal delays. This is known as *modal dispersion*. Obviously, this is highly undesirable in ultrafast digital transmission, where pulses may be as narrow as a few tens of picoseconds. The difference in travel time is improved if, for example, a single mode graded-index fiber is used.

1.7.2 Chromatic Dispersion

The refractive index of the material is related to the dielectric coefficient ϵ and to the characteristic resonant frequencies of its dipoles. Thus, the dipoles interact stronger with optical frequencies that are closer to their resonant frequencies. Consequently, the refractive index $n(\omega)$ is optical frequency dependent, and it affects the propagation characteristics of each frequency (or wavelength) in the signal differently.

An optical signal is not strictly monochromatic, but it consists of a continuum of wavelengths in a narrow spectral range. The propagation characteristics of each wavelength in the optical signal depend on the refractive index of the medium and the nonlinearity of the propagation constant. These dependencies affect the travel time of each wavelength in the signal through a fiber medium. As a result, an initially narrow pulse is widened because the pulse is not monochromatic but in reality it consists of a group of wavelengths (Figure 1.3). This is termed *chromatic dispersion*.

Silica, a key ingredient of optical fiber cable, has a refractive index that varies with optical frequency. Therefore, dispersion plays a significant role in fiber-optic communications. The dependence on wavelength λ also causes dispersion known as *wavelength dispersion*. The part of chromatic dispersion that depends on the dielectric constant ϵ is known as *material dispersion*. Material dispersion is the most significant. Dispersion is measured in picoseconds per nanometer-kilometer (i.e., delay per wavelength variation and fiber length).

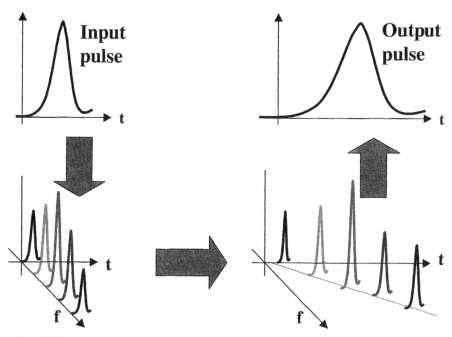

Figure 1.3 Chromatic dispersion: from input to output pulse.

1.7.3 Polarization Mode Dispersion

As already discussed, birefringence causes an optical (monochromatic) signal to be separated in two orthogonally polarized signals, each traveling at different speed. The same occurs if an optical pulse of a modulated optical signal travels in a birefringent fiber or in a birefringent component; the pulse is separated into two pulses, each traveling at different speeds with different polarization. Thus, when the two signals recombine, because of the variation in time of arrival, a pulse spreading occurs. This phenomenon is known as *polarization mode dispersion* (PMD) and is noticeable in ultrahigh bit rates (above 2.5 Gbps).

Optical fibers have a polarization mode dispersion coefficient of less than 0.5 ps/km$^{1/2}$ (see ITU-T G.652, G.653, and G.655). For an STS-192/STM-64 signal (~10 Gbps), this PMD coefficient value limits the fiber length to 400 km.

1.8 FIBER ATTENUATION AND LOSS

Optical loss of a fiber, also known as *fiber attenuation,* is a very important transmission characteristic that has a limiting effect on the fiber span, as it imposes power *loss* on the optical signal. That is, for a given launched optical power $P(0)$

into the fiber, attenuation affects the total power P_r arrived at the receiver and, in order to meet the specified signal quality level, it limits the fiber span L_{max} if there is no amplification.

Fiber attenuation depends on scattering mechanisms, on fluctuations of the refractive index, on fiber imperfections, and on impurities. Conventional single-mode fibers have two low attenuation ranges, one about 1.3 μm and another about 1.55 μm. Metal ions and OH radicals have a particular attenuation effect at about 1.4 μm, although fiber almost free of OH radicals has been successfully manufactured. The AllWave$^{(TM)}$ fiber by Lucent Technologies has a low water peak (LWPF) with minimum attenuation over the entire spectrum between 1310 and 1625 nm. In DWDM, this corresponds to about 500 channels with 100 GHz channel spacing.

Fiber attenuation is measured in decibels per kilometer. ITU-T G.652 recommends losses below 0.5 dB/km in the region 1310 nm and below 0.4 dB/km in the region 1500 nm. Some typical values are 0.4 dB/km at about 1310 nm and 0.2 dB/km at about 1550 nm.

1.9 FIBER SPECTRUM UTILIZATION

1.9.1 Spectral Bands

Based on optical power loss in fiber and the spectral performance of optical devices, a number of spectrum ranges have been characterized for compatibility purposes with light sources, receivers, and optical components, including the fiber. Thus, the low-loss spectrum for conventional single-mode fibers has been subdivided into three usable regions as follows:

Band	Wavelength Range (nm)
S-band (short wavelength or second window)	1280–1350
C-band (conventional or third window)	1528–1561
L-band (long wavelength or fourth window)	1561–1660

1.9.2 ITU-T C-Band Nominal Center Frequencies

ITU-T G.692 (October 1998) has recommended 81 optical channels in the C-band with the first channel centered at 196.10 THz (1528.77 nm). Subsequent channels are determined by decrementing by 50 GHz (or incrementing by 0.39 nm). The last channel is centered at 192.10 THz (1560.61 nm). These frequencies are determined from a reference frequency set at 193.10 THz (or 1552.52 nm).

For a channel spacing of 100 GHz, the nominal frequencies are those that start with the first channel in the table (196.10 THz) and continue every other one; similarly, for channel spacing of 200 GHz is every four channels and for 400 GHz is every eight.

The nominal frequency of each channel in the range 196.10–192.10 THz is calculated according to

$$F = 196.10 - ms \quad \text{(THz)}$$

where $m = 1, 2, \ldots$ and $s = 0.050, 0.100, 0.200, 0.400$ THz, or

$$F = 193.10 \pm ms \quad \text{(THz)}$$

where $m = 0, 1, 2, \ldots$ and $s = 0.050, 0.100, 0.200, 0.400$ THz.

1.10 NONLINEAR PHENOMENA

When light enters matter, photons and atoms interact, and under certain circumstances, photons may be absorbed by atoms and excite them to higher energy levels.

When atoms are excited to a higher state, they do not remain stable. Photons passing by may stimulate them to come down to their initial lower energy level by releasing energy, *photons* and *phonons* (the acoustic quantum equivalent of light).

The behavior of dielectric molecules to optical power is like a dipole. It is the dipole nature of a dielectric that interacts harmonically with electromagnetic waves such as light. When the optical power is low, it results in small oscillations that approximate the photon-fiber system linear behavior. However, when the optical power is large, the oscillations are such that higher order terms (nonlinear behavior) become significant.

In addition to the phenomena from the photon-atom interaction, there are also photon-atom-photon interactions that result in some complex phenomena, some of them not well understood yet. These interactions are distinguished in *forward scattering* and in *backward scattering* [Raman scattering (SRS) and Brillouin (SBS) scattering] as well as in *four-wave (or four-photon) mixing* (FWM). The direction (forward and backward) is with respect to the direction of the excitation light.

In optical systems, nonlinear phenomena are viewed as both advantageous and degrading:

- *Advantageous,* because lasers, optical amplifiers, and dispersion compensation are based on them

- *Degrading,* because signal losses, noise, cross-talk, and pulse broadening are caused by them

1.11 SPECTRAL BROADENING

The refractive index of many materials depends on the amplitude of the electrical field. Thus, as the electrical field changes, so does the refractive index. However, refractive index variations impact the transmission characteristics of the signal itself.

As an almost monochromatic light pulse travels through a fiber, its amplitude variation causes *phase change* and *spectral broadening*. Phase variations are equivalent to frequency modulation or "chirping." Spectral broadening appears as if one-half of the frequency is downshifted (known as *red shift*) and as if the other half is upshifted (known as *blue shift*). Such shifts are also expected in pulses that consist of a narrow range of wavelengths and are centered at the zero-dispersion wavelength. Below the zero-dispersion point *wavelength dispersion is negative and above it is positive*. Because of this, the zero-dispersion point is avoided and the operating point is preferred to be in the positive or in the negative dispersion area.

1.12 SELF-PHASE MODULATION

The dynamic characteristics of a propagating light pulse in a fiber result in modulation of its own phase, due to the Kerr effect of the fiber medium. According to this phenomenon, known as *self-phase modulation,* spectral broadening may also take place.

Specifically, if the wavelength of the pulse is below the zero-dispersion point (known as *normal dispersion regime*), then spectral broadening causes temporal broadening of the pulse as it propagates. If, on the other hand, the wavelength is above the zero-dispersion wavelength of the fiber (the *anomalous dispersion regime*), then chromatic dispersion and self-phase modulation compensate for each other, thus reducing temporal broadening.

1.13 SELF-MODULATION OR MODULATION INSTABILITY

When a single pulse of an almost monochromatic light has a wavelength above the zero-dispersion wavelength of the fiber (the anomalous dispersion regime), another phenomenon occurs that degrades the width of the pulse, known as *self-modulation* or *modulation instability*. According to this, two side-lobe pulses are symmetrically generated at either side of the original pulse.

Modulation instability affects the signal-to-noise ratio, and it is considered a special FWM case. Modulation instability is reduced by operating at low energy levels and/or at wavelengths below the zero-dispersion wavelength.

1.14 EFFECTS OF TEMPERATURE ON MATTER AND LIGHT

The properties of materials vary as temperature varies. In addition to changing its physical properties, the optical, electrical, magnetic, and chemical properties change as well. As a result, the crystaline structure of matter is affected as well as its dielectric constant and the index of refraction. Clearly, in optical communications, adverse changes on the propagation parameters affect the optical signal and its quality, its signal-to-noise ratio, and thus the bit error rate (BER). Therefore, temperature variations are undesirable, although there are cases where this has been used productively to control optical devices by varying the temperature and thus the refractive index. In subsequent chapters we study the effect of parametric changes on the quality of the optical signal.

1.15 LIGHT ATTRIBUTES

Light consists of many frequencies. Its power may be split, coupled, reflected, refracted, diffracted, absorbed, scattered, and polarized. Light interacts with matter, and it even interacts with itself. Light is immune to radio frequency (RF) electromagnetic interference (EMI). The attributes of light are given below:

Light Attributes	Comments
Dual nature	Electromagnetic wave and particle
Consists of many λ's	Within a very wide and continuous spectrum Under certain circumstances, its frequency may be changed to another
Propagation	Follows a straight path in free space* Follows the bends of optical waveguides Its speed depends on the refractive index of matter Affected by refractive index variations
Polarization	Circular, Elliptic, Linear (TE_{nm}, TM_{nm}) Polarization is affected by fields Polarization is affected by matter
Optical power	Wide range (from less than microwatts to watts)[†]
Propagation speed	Fastest possible (in free space $c \sim 10^{10}$ cm/s, in matter c/n)
Phase	Affected by field discontinuities Affected by material constants
Optical channel	A narrow band of optical frequencies is modulated Ultrafast modulation (many gigahertz) possible May be contaminated by additive optical spectral noise

*Undisturbed light travels forever. In matter, it travels the shortest possible path.
[†]Here, we consider optical power in fiber communications.

Cause	Effect
λ's interact among themselves	Interference, new wavelength generation
λ's interact with matter	Range of effects (e.g., absorption, scattering, reflection, refraction, diffraction, polarization, polarization shift) Nonlinear effects (e.g., FWM)
Each λ interacts with matter differently	Range of effects (e.g., dispersion, PMD)
λ-matter-λ interaction	Birefringence, phase shift, modulation issues, SRS, SBS, optical fiber amplifiers (OFAs); possible wavelength conversion
No purely monochromatic (single-λ) channel	Finite number of channels within spectrum

1.16 MATERIAL ATTRIBUTES

Not all optical materials interact with light in the same manner. Materials with specific desirable optical properties have been used to device optical compo-

Material Attributes	Comments
Refractive index (n)	A function of molecular structure of matter A function of optical frequency A function of optical intensity Determines optical propagation properties of each λ Affected by external temperature, pressure, and fields
Flat surface reflectivity (R)	A function of molecular/atomic structure, λ and n Affects the reflected power (also a function of angle) Changes the polarization of incident wave Changes the phase of incident optical wave
Transparency (T)	Depends on material consistency and parameters
Scattering	Mainly due to molecular matrix disorders and contaminants
Absorption (A)	Mainly due to ions in the matrix and other contaminants
Polarization (P)	Due to X-Y uneven electromagnetic (EM) fields (light-matter interaction)
Birefringence (B)	Due to nonuniform distribution of n in all directions
Phase shift ($\Delta\Phi$)	Due to wave property of light through matter
Ions act like dipoles	Exhibit eigenfrequencies Exhibit antenna characteristics (receiver/transmitter)

nents. In some cases, artificially made materials have been manufactured to produce desirable properties. Here we examine certain key atributes of optical materials.

Cause	Effect
Refractive index variation (n)	May not be the same in all directions within matter
	Affects the propagation of light
	Responsible for birefringence, dispersion, and dichroism
Transparency variation	Affects the amount of light passing through matter
Scattering	Photonic power loss (attenuation)
Absorption	Photonic power loss, SRS, SBS, OFA
Reflectivity	Material surface reflects optical power
	Changes polarization of incident optical wave
	Changes phase of incident optical wave
Polarization	Mode change: circular, elliptic, linear (TE_{nm}, TM_{nm})
	Affects power received
Birefringence	Splits light in two different rays and directions (ordinary and extraordinary)
Phase shift (PS)	Optical PS may be desirable or undesirable
	Undesirable in transmission, desirable when it is controlled
Ions act like EM dipoles	Interact selectively with light waves
	Responsible for energy absorption or energy exchange
	Change propagation characteristics (speed, phase) of λ's
	Affect the refractive index
	Nonlinear phenomena (SRS, SBS, FWM)

1.17 MEASURABLE PARAMETERS

Optical parameters are measured with instruments, some small and compact and some very complex and impractical, as they are seen from a communications system point of view. In addition, some instruments are beyond conventional knowledge and require extensive and specialized knowledge of optics. Therefore, the in-system optical parameter monitors for detecting degradations and faults may require instrumentation or measuring methods that may or may not be cost-ineffective. However, if many resources share a measuring method, then the added cost per optical channel (OCh) may be low. In addition, when a measuring method requires non-evasive optical monitoring then, the optical power penalty imposed by the method can be minimal.

Photonic Parameters	Detectability*
Center wavelength (λ_0) of an optical channel (nm)	Spectrum analyzer
Line witdth ($\Delta\lambda$, nm, or GHz)	Spectrum analyzer
Line spacing or channel separation ($\Delta\lambda$, GHz, or nm)	Spectrum analyzer
Power amplitude at λ_0 ($P_{\lambda 0}$, mW)	Filter plus photodetector
Launched optical power (P_{launched}, mW)	Backscattered photodetector
Received optical power (P_{received}, mW)	Filter plus photodetector
Insertion loss (L, dB)	Calculate ratio P_O/P_1
Polarization, degree of (DOP, %)	Complex
Polarization-dependent loss (PDL) (dB)	Complex
Direction of propagation (Cartesian or polar coordinates)	Complex
Speed of light (v)	Complex
Group velocity (v_g)	Complex
Propagation constant (β)	Complex

*"Complex" denotes, based on current techniques, a nontrivial optoelectronic set-up.

Parameters Due to Light-Matter Interaction	Calculability/Detectability
Attenuation ($-$dB)	$A\lambda = 10 \log[P_{\text{out}}(\lambda)/P_{\text{in}}(\lambda)]$, $P_{\text{in}} > P_{\text{out}}$
Attenuation coefficient (dB/km)	$\alpha(\lambda) = A(\lambda)/L$; provided by manufacturer's specifications
Insertion loss ($-$dB)	$L_{ij} = -10 \log_{10}t_{ij}$ or $L_{ij} = P_j - P_I$; $t_{ij} =$ input/output (I/O) power transfer
Amplification gain (dB)	$g(\lambda) = 10 \log[P_{\text{out}}(\lambda)/P_{\text{in}}(\lambda)]$, $P_{\text{in}} < P_{\text{out}}$
Birefringence	P_O/P_E; indirectly (BER, cross-talk)
Extinction ratio	P_B/P_F; indirectly from IL and $A(\lambda)$
Pulse spreading (ps)	Indirectly: eye diagram, BER, cross-talk
Group delay (ps)*	$\tau(\lambda) = \tau 0 + (S_0/2)(\lambda - \lambda_0)^{2\dagger}$
Differential group delay (ps/km$^{1/2}$)	See ITU G.650 for procedure
Chromatic dispersion coefficient (ps/nm-km)*	$D(\lambda) = S_0(\lambda - \lambda_0)$
Polarization mode dispersion (ps/km$^{1/2}$)	Requires laboratory optical set-up
Phase shift ($\Delta\phi$)	Interferometry
Polarization mode shift	Requires laboratory optical set-up
Dispersion effects	See pulse spreading

Note: P_O and P_E: optical power in the ordinary and extraordinary directions, respectively; P_B and P_F: optical power in the backward and in the forward directions, respectively.
*Relationship depends on fiber type (see ITU-T G.652, G.653, G.654).
$^\dagger S_0$ is the zero-dispersion slope.

REFERENCES

[1] M. H. Freeman, *Optics,* 10th ed., Butterworths, London, 1990.

[2] W. H. A. Fincham and M. H. Freeman, *Optics,* Butterworths, London, 1974.

[3] E. B. Brown, *Modern Optics,* Reinhold, New York, 1965.

[4] A. Kastler, *Optique,* 6th ed., Masson & Cie, Paris, 1965.

[5] K. Nassau, *The Physics and Chemistry of Color,* Wiley, New York, 1983.

[6] H. A. Haus, *Waves and Fields in Optoelectronics,* Prentice-Hall, Englewood Cliffs, NJ, 1984.

[7] T. Wildi, *Units and Conversion Charts,* 2nd ed., IEEE Press, New York, 1995.

[8] R. G. Hunsperger, *Integrated Optics: Theory and Technology,* Springer-Verlag, New York, 1984.

[9] L. Desmarais, *Applied Electro-Optics,* Prentice-Hall, Englewood Cliffs, NJ, 1999.

[10] J. Nellist, *Understanding Telecommunications and Lightwave Systems,* IEEE Press, New York, 1996.

[11] J. Hecht, *Understanding Fiber Optics,* Prentice-Hall, Englewood Cliffs, NJ, 1999.

[12] E. B. Carne, *Telecommunications Primer,* Prentice-Hall, Englewood Cliffs, NJ, 1995.

[13] P. S. Henry, "Lightwave Primer," *IEEE J. Quant. Electron.,* vol. QE-21, 1985, pp. 1862–1879.

[14] J. J. Refi, "Optical Fibers for Optical Networking," *Bell Labs. Tech. J.,* vol. 4, no. 1, 1999, pp. 246–261.

[15] L. Kazovsky, S. Benedetto, and A. Willner, *Optical Fiber Communication Systems,* Artech House, Boston, 1996.

[16] B. Mukherjee, *Optical Communication Networks,* McGraw-Hill, New York, 1997.

[17] J. C. Palais, *Fiber Optic Communications,* 3rd ed., Prentice-Hall, Englewood Cliffs, NJ, 1992.

[18] S. V. Kartalopoulos, *Understanding SONET/SDH and ATM: Communications Networks for the Next Millennium,* IEEE Press, New York, 1999.

[19] S. V. Kartalopoulos, *Introduction to DWDM Technology: Data in a Rainbow,* IEEE Press, New York, 2000.

[20] H. Toba and K. Nosu, "Optical Frequency Division Multiplexing System-Review of Key Technologies and Applications," *IEICE Trans. Comm.,* vol. E75-B, no. 4, Apr. 1992, pp. 243–255

[21] J. R. Freer, *Computer Communications and Networks,* IEEE Press, New York, 1996.

[22] S. R. Nagle, "Optical Fiber—The Expanding Medium," *IEEE Circuits Devices Mag.,* vol. 5, no. 2, 1989, pp. 36–45.

[23] R. H. Stolen, "Non-Linear Properties of Optical Fibers," in *Optical Fiber Telecommunications,* S. E. Miller and G. Chynoweth, Eds., Academic, New York, 1979.

[24] F. Ouellette, "All-Fiber for Efficient Dispersion Compensation," *Opt. Lett.,* vol. 16, no. 5, 1991, pp. 303–304.

[25] S. E. Miller, "Coupled-Wave Theory and Waveguide Applications," *Bell Syst. Tech. J.,* vol. 33, 1954, pp. 661–719.

[26] A. Yariv, "Coupled Mode Theory for Guided Wave Optics," *IEEE J. Quant. Electron.*, vol QE-9, 1973, pp. 919–933.

[27] R. Driggers, P. Cox, and T. Edwards, *An Introduction to Infrared and Electro-Optical Systems,* Artech House, Boston, 1999.

[28] N. Shibata, K. Nosu, K. Iwashita, and Y. Azuma, "Transmission Limitations Due to Fiber Nonlinearities in Optical FDM Systems," *IEEE J. Selected Areas Commun.*, vol. 8, no. 6, 1990, pp. 1068–1077.

[29] S. V. Kartalopoulos, "A Plateau of Performance?" Guest Editorial, *IEEE Commun. Mag.*, Sept. 1992, pp. 13–14.

STANDARDS

[1] ANSI/IEEE 812-1984, "Definition of Terms Relating to Fiber Optics," 1984.

[2] IEC Publication 793-2, Part 2, "Optical Fibres—Part 2: Product Specifications," 1992.

[3] ITU-T Recommendation G.652, version 4, "Characteristics of a Single-Mode Optical Fiber Cable," Apr. 1997.

[4] ITU-T Recommendation G.653, version 4, "Characteristics of a Dispersion-Shifted Single-Mode Optical Fiber Cable," Apr. 1997.

[5] ITU-T Recommendation G.654, "Characteristics of a Cut-off Shifted Single-Mode Optical Fibre Cable," 1997.

[6] ITU-T Recommendation G.655, version 10, "Characteristics of a Non-Zero Dispersion-Shifted Single-Mode Optical Fiber Cable," Oct. 1996.

[7] ITU-T Recommendation G.662, "Generic Characteristics of Optical Fiber Amplifier Devices and Sub-Systems," July 1995.

[8] ITU-T Recommendation G.671, "Transmission Characteristics of Passive Optical Components," Nov. 1996.

[9] ITU-T Recommendation G.702, "Digital Hierarchy Bit Rates," 1988.

[10] ITU-T Recommendation G.821, "Error Performance of an International Digital Connection Operating at a Bit Rate Below the Primary Rate and Forming Part of an Integrated Services Digital Network," Aug. 1996.

[11] ITU-T Recommendation G.826, "Error Performance Parameters and Objectives for International, Constant Bit Rate Digital Paths at or Above the Primary Rate," Feb. 1999.

[12] ITU-T Recommendation G.828, "Error Performance Parameters and Objectives for International, Constant Bit Rate Synchronous Digital Paths," Feb. 2000.

[13] Go to http://www.itu.int/ITU-T/index.html, for more information on ITU standards.

CHAPTER 2

OPTICAL COMPONENTS

2.1 INTRODUCTION

The four key components in optical communications systems are the monochromatic light source, the light modulator, the optical fiber, and the photodetector or receiver. However, the key components in DWDM optical communications systems, in addition to the aforementioned, are filters, optical multiplexers and demultiplexers, optical switches, and optical amplifiers.

In optical communications, optical components should be compact, monochromatic, or polychromatic (as required) and stable over their life span. Stability implies constant output power level (over time and temperature variations) and no wavelength drifting.

2.2 LASER SOURCES

Laser stands for light amplification by stimulated emission radiation. It has been found that some elements in gaseous state (e.g., He-Ne) and some in solid state (e.g., ruby with 0.05% chromium) absorb electromagnetic energy (light) and remain in a semistable high-energy excited state for a short period. This high-energy state can then be stimulated in a controllable manner to emit light of specific wavelengths at a variety of power levels.

This property of certain materials is used to construct a laser source. When the material is excited, traveling photons interact with it in the electron-hole recombination region whereby a cascaded and rapid process is triggered by which excited atoms drop from their high-energy state to a low-energy state by releasing energy in the form of light; that is, a single photon causes many. Photons are created in a region known as the cavity where they are reflected back and forth (in phase) to form a *coherent* monochromatic beam; photons traveling in other directions are eventually lost through the walls of the cavity. As energy is pumped in, the emitted photons are replenished, and the optical gain reaches a threshold and the lasing process starts. The lasing property of certain organic materials in crystal phase have also been demonstrated.

Lasers that support a *single transversal mode* are known as *single-mode* (whether they oscillate in a single or multiple longitudinal modes). Those that support both a *single transversal mode* and a *single longitudinal mode* are known as *single-frequency lasers*. If they oscillate at *several frequencies simultaneously,* longitudinal or transversal, then, they are called *multifrequency lasers*.

Lasers can be directly modulated. However, direct modulation at very high bit rates (10–40 Gbps) has an unpleasant effect. As the drive current changes from logic 1 to logic 0 and vice versa, the refractive index of the laser cavity changes dynamically (effectively changing the resonant cavity characteristics), which causes dynamic change in wavelength, and hence *optical chirping;* that is, a form of wavelength jitter and noise. Chirping is undesirable, and to avoid it, external modulation is used, in which case the laser emits a continuous wave (CW). However, since lasers and modulators can be made with In+Ga+As+P, then, they can both be monolithically integrated on an InP substrate to yield a compact device.

Wavelength and signal amplitude stability of semiconductor lasers is important in efficient transmission. Stability depends on materials, bias voltage, and temperature (Figure 2.1). Usually frequency stabilization is established using thermoelectric cooling techniques that keep the temperature stable within a fraction of a degree Celsius. However, this adds to the cost structure and power consumption of the device, and efforts are made to design "cooler" devices.

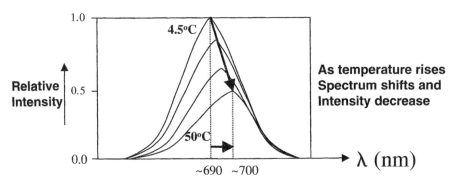

Figure 2.1 Spectral output depends on the absolute junction temperature.

2.2.1 Single-Frequency Lasers

Single-frequency lasers are tuned by controlling the refractive index. In this case, the index of refraction in the lasing cavity is varied so that the peak transmissivity of the intracavity filter shifts to yield the desired wavelength. Changing the refractive index is equivalent to increasing the length of a free-space cavity. (Why?)

2.2.2 Multifrequency Lasers

Multifrequency lasers are classified as integrated cavity lasers and arrayed lasers.

Integrated cavity lasers have an integrated cavity, whereby the cavity serves both as a filter and as a multiport optical power combiner (multiplexer). This laser may also be integrated with optical amplifiers.

Arrayed lasers are integrated arrays of individually tuned-frequency lasers and their outputs are combined to produce the range of desired frequencies. In this category are the distributed-feedback (DFB) arrays. An array of DFB lasers may also be used as a wavelength-selectable device. In this case, several DFB lasers are monolithically integrated, each generating a different wavelength. Then, one of the DFB lasers is selected, the one that generates the wavelength of interest. If each DFB laser has its own modulator, then a multiwavelength source is generated.

2.3 OPTICAL COMB GENERATORS

An optical comb generator is a device that generates a predetermined range of $2K + 1$ distinct wavelengths with a predetermined spacing Ω when an angle modulated optical signal $Y(t)$ is applied, described by

$$Y(t) = A_S \cos(\omega t + m \sin \Omega t)$$

where A_S is the signal amplitude, ω is the optical frequency, m is the modulation index, and Ω is the modulation frequency.

The above relationship indicates that the power of the applied signal $Y(t)$ spreads among a spectrum of several frequencies that consists of the fundamental frequency and sidebands.

The total number of components in the comb depends on the value of m. For example, for $m = 3$, there are seven terms, one fundamental and three sidebands on each side. The output spectrum of a comb is described by

$$S(f) = \Sigma \, A_k \delta(f - k\Omega) \qquad -K < k < K$$

where A_k is the amplitude of the kth component and $\delta(f - k\Omega)$ is the frequency member of the comb represented by a delta function. Ideally, all A_k values should be identical; in reality, they are not due to an amplitude modulation (filtering) effect.

2.4 CHIRPED-PULSE LASER SOURCES

A different method that generates many wavelengths from a very narrow pulse is known as chirped-pulse wavelength-division multiplexing (CPWDM). To explain this, consider a high-power and very narrow pulse (femtoseconds wide) coupled in a highly dispersive fiber. Due to dispersion, the pulse is broadened to nanoseconds while spreading the spectral frequency content of the light, equivalent to Fourier analysis, based on which many frequency components are generated from a single impulse; the narrower the impulse, the more the frequency content. This method is known as "chirping." Now, consider a mode-locked laser source that emits a sequence of ultrashort pulses. Thus, each pulse generates a set of pulsed frequencies in the time-spectrum continuum, each pulse referred to as a slice. Time-division multiplexed data (via a fast modulator) modulate the bits of every slice and thus each frequency channel is modulated with different data.

2.5 MODULATORS

Optical modulators are components designed to control a property of light that passes through them. They are devices positioned in line with a CW laser source (external modulation) or they are monolithically integrated with a laser source (direct modulation). The major benefit of external modulators is that they have negligible chirp (phase jitter), as compared with direct modulation; chirp and fiber dispersion effects limit the transmission distance of the source detector.

As an optical (monochromatic) beam passes through a modulator, one of its following properties changes:

- Intensity
- Phase
- Frequency
- Polarization

The parameters that characterize the performance of optical modulators are as follows:

- Modulation depth η
- Modulation format (analog/digital, linear/nonlinear)
- Percent modulation (typical in intensity modulators)
- Bandwidth
- Insertion loss
- Degree of isolation
- Power

1. For *intensity modulators:* In this category are the electroabsorption (EA) modulators. Electroabsorption modulators exhibit an almost logarithmic optical power attenuation, which depends on the voltage applied to them, thus acting as on-off optical devices. They are sources of short optical pulses (and short duty cycle), they exhibit excellent modulation depths in excess of 45 dB, and they can generate

bit rates in excess of 40 Gbps. They are made with InGaAsP and thus are compact and stable devices that can easily be integrated with other optical devices (e.g., DFB lasers).

    a. The *modulation depth* is defined by $\eta = (I_0 - I)/I_0$.

    b. The *extinction ratio* is the maximum value of η, η_{max}, when the intensity of the transmitted beam is a minimum, I_{min}, and it is given by $\eta_{max} = \eta(I_{min})$.

  2. For *phase modulators* the modulation depth η is defined similarly provided that the intensity is related to the phase [$I = I(\phi)$].

  3. For *frequency modulators* an analogous figure of merit is used known as the maximum frequency deviation D_{max}, defined as $D_{max} = \left| f_m - f_0 \right| / f_0$, where f_m is the maximum frequency shift of the carrier f_0.

The *degree of isolation,* in decibels, represents the maximum optical change produced by the modulator and is related to the extinction ratio [$10 \log(\eta)$] or to the maximum frequency deviation ($10 \log D_{max}$).

2.6 PHOTODETECTORS

Photodetectors (or photosensors) are transducers that alter one of their characteristics in a relationship relative to the amount of light energy that impinges on them. Thus, *photoresistors* alter their ohmic resistance, *rods* and *cones,* neurons of the retina of the eye alter their electrochemical response, chlorophyll in plant leaves alter the rate of converting CO_2 to O_2, and semiconductor photodetectors alter the flow of electrical current or the potential difference across their two terminals.

Photodetectors with sufficiently fast response (picoseconds) that provide a measurable output for a small amount of light, that are easily reproducible, and that are economical are the primary candidates in high-speed optical communication applications. In this category are the avalanche photodiodes (APDs) and the positive-intrinsic-negative (PIN) diodes.

Photodetectors are characterized by certain key parameters. Among them are the *spectral response, photosensitivity, quantum efficiency, dark current, forward-biased noise, noise-equivalent power, terminal capacitance, timing response* (rise time and fall time), *frequency bandwidth,* and *cutoff frequency:*

- Spectral response relates the amount of current produced with wavelength, assuming all wavelengths are at the same level of light.

- Photosensitivity is the ratio of light energy (in watts) incident on the device to the resulting current (in amperes).

- Quantum efficiency is the number of generated electron-holes (i.e., current) divided by the number of photons.

- Dark current is the amount of current that flows through the photodiode in the absence of any light (dark), when the diode is reverse biased. This becomes a source of noise when the diode is reversed biased.

- Forward-biased noise is a (current) source of noise that is related to the shunt resistance of the device. The shunt resistance is defined as the ratio voltage (near 0 V) over the amount of current generated. This is also called *shunt resistance* noise.

- Noise-equivalent power is defined as the amount of light (of a given wavelength) that is equivalent to the noise level of the device.

- Terminal capacitance is the capacitance from the *p-n* junction of the diode to the connectors of the device; it limits the response of the photodetector.

- The timing response of the photodetector is defined as the time lapsed for the output signal to reach from 10 to 90% of its amplitude (rise time) and from 90 to 10% (fall time).

- Frequency bandwidth is defined as the frequency (or wavelength) range in which the photodetector is sensitive.

- Cutoff frequency is the highest frequency (wavelength) to which the photodetector is sensitive.

2.7   FIXED OPTICAL FILTERS

The function of a filter is to recognize a narrow band of electrical frequencies from a multiplicity and either pass it or reject it. Optical spectral filters are based on *interference* or on *absorption* and they are distinguished in *fixed* and in *tunable* filters.

Filters are characterized by several parameters:

- *Spectral width* is defined as the band of frequencies that will pass through the filter. The spectral width is characterized by an upper and by a lower frequency (wavelength) threshold. In addition, it is characterized by a gain curve that is a measure of the degree of flatness over the spectral width.

- *Line width* or *channel width* is defined as the width of the frequency channel. An ideal channel should be monochromatic, that is, a single wavelength. However, this is not possible, and thus the line width is a measure of how close to ideal a channel is, as well as an indication of the spectral content of the channel.

- *Line spacing* is defined as the distance in wavelength units (nanometers) or in frequency units (gigahertz) between two channels.

- *Finesse* is an indication of how many wavelength (or frequency) channels can simultaneously pass through the filter without severe interference among them. The finesse is a measure of the energy of wavelengths within the cavity relative to the energy lost per cycle. Thus, the higher the finesse, the narrower the resonant line width. The Q-factor of electrical filters is equivalent to the finesse.

Cavity losses due to imperfections of mirrors (e.g., flatness) and angle of incidence of the light beam impact the finesse value. Usually, the finesse is dominated by reflector losses due to power that flows in and out as a result of the semitransparency of the filter reflectors.

2.7.1 Fabry-Perot Filter

The Fabry-Perot filter is based on the interference of multiple reflections of a light beam by two surfaces of a thin plate (Figure 2.2). It consists of two high-reflectance semireflectors separated by a distance d. Multiple interference in the space layer causes the filter output spectral characteristic to peak sharply over a narrow band of wavelengths that are multiple of the $\lambda/2$ spacer layer. The condition for interference maxima for each wavelength is $2d \sin \Theta = n\lambda$, where n is an integer. The values of λ that satisfy the relationship $\lambda = 2dn/m$ determine the *modes* of the Fabry-Perot filter. As an example, for $m = 1$ and $n = 1$, $\lambda = 2d$; for $m = 2$ and $n = 1$, $l = d$. Thus, a Fabry-Perot filter is used exclusively as a bandpass filter.

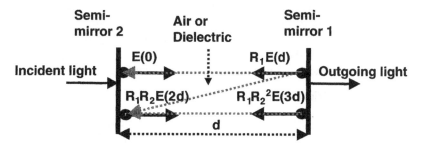

Figure 2.2 Principles of the Fabry-Perot interferometer.

2.7.2 Bragg Grating Filter

The Bragg *grating* is an arrangement of multiple parallel semireflecting plates (Figure 2.3). In this arrangement the condition for total reflection is derived in the form of a geometric series when one calculates the sum of all reflected components at the first mirror and assuming that all waves arrive in phase. Then, this sum yields the *condition for strong reflection* or *Bragg condition* $d = -n \lambda_B/2$. The negative sign denotes reflection and n is the order of the Bragg grating. When $n = 1$ (first order), $d = \lambda/2$, and when $n = 2$ (second order), $d = \lambda$.

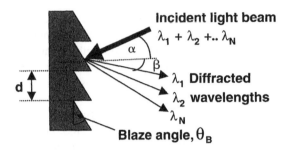

Figure 2.3 Principles of the diffraction grating; shown are the blaze angle and the grating period.

A *fiber Bragg grating* (FBG) consists of a fiber segment whose index of refraction varies periodically along its length. Fiber Bragg gratings with a variable pitch may compensate for chromatic dispersion, known as chirped-FBGs.

A similar Bragg grating reflector is based on a stack of dielectric layers, known as *photonic lattice*. The layers are quarter-wavelength thick and with different refractive indices. Photonic lattice reflectors have been found to reflect wavelengths, in the spectral band it is designed for, over all possible angles of incidence, and they do not absorb any of the incident energy, as mirror-based reflectors do.

2.7.3 Mach-Zehnder Filter

The *Mach-Zehnder* filter is based on the interference of two coherent monochromatic sources that, based on the length difference and thus the phase difference of the two paths, contribute positively or negatively. However, one should remember that since optical channels are not purely monochromatic, the polychromatic nature of each optical channel should be taken into account when calculating the minima (destructive interference) and maxima (constructive interference) of light.

2.7.4 Dielectric Thin-Film Filter

Dielectric thin-film (DTF) interference filters consist of alternate layers of high refractive index and low refractive index, each layer being $\lambda/4$ thick. Light of specified λ and reflected within the layers of high index does not shift its phase, whereas those within the low index shift by 180°. Taking into account the travel difference (in multiples of $2 \times \lambda/4$), reflected light recombines constructively at the front face, producing a highly reflected beam with wavelengths in a narrow range. Outside this range the wavelengths drop abruptly at the output of the filter.

The primary considerations in DTF design are as follows:

- Low passband loss
- Good channel spacing
- Low interchannel cross-talk

The wavelength range at the output of the $\lambda/4$ stack depends on the ratio of high to low refractive index. Thus, a DTF can be used as a high-pass filter, a low-pass filter, or a high-reflectance layer. Low passband loss is achieved with multilayer structures that exceed 98% reflectance. Clearly, any external influence that may alter the parameters of a DFT will also alter the filter characteristics.

2.7.5 Quarter-Wavelength and Half-Wavelength Plates

A birefringent plate of a quarter-wavelength ($\lambda/4$) thickness and with the surfaces parallel to the optic axis has important properties on polarized light.

If the linear-polarized light is at 45° to the fast optical axis, the polarization is transformed into circular-polarized light, and vice versa.

If the linear-polarized light is parallel to the fast or slow axis, the polarization remains unchanged.

If the linear-polarized light is at any other angle with the optical axis, linear polarization is transformed into elliptical polarization and vice versa.

Similar to $\lambda/4$ plates, a half-wavelength plate with the surfaces parallel to the optic axis has other important properties on polarized light.

If the linear-polarized light is at $\theta°$ to the fast optical axis, the polarization remains linear but the orientation is rotated by $2\theta°$. Thus, if the angle is 45°, the linear polarization is rotated by 90°.

2.8 TUNABLE OPTICAL FILTERS

Tunable optical filters (TOFs) may be constructed with passive or active optical components. The salient characteristic of TOFs is their ability to select the range of filtered wavelengths. However, to be useful in optical communication systems, they must satisfy certain requirements:

- Wide tuning range (large number of channels)
- Constant gain (over the filter spectrum)
- Narrow bandwidth
- Fast tuning
- Insensitivity to temperature (no frequency drift with temperature variations)

Each tunable filter type has its own performance characteristics. Therefore, depending on the application, the filter type that best matches the performance requirements should be used.

2.8.1 Acousto-Optic Tunable Filters

Acousto-optic tunable optical filters (AOTFs) are based on the Bragg principle according to which only those wavelengths pass through the filter that comply with the Bragg condition. The index of refraction is made to fluctuate periodically by applying a radio-frequency (RF) acoustical signal to an optically transparent waveguide. The applied RF disturbs its molecular structure with a periodicity that determines the periodicity of the index of refraction. Thus, the polarization of the optical wavelength that complies with the Bragg condition is rotated from TE to TM.

AOTF filters are used in single-wavelength tunable receivers, multiwavelength tunable receivers, and wavelength-selective space switches (demultiplexers). A disadvantage of typical AOTFs is the misalignment of the polarization state of incoming light. Polarization mismatch results in coupling loss. Another disadvantage is a frequency shift by an amount equal to the acoustical frequency due to the Doppler effect. However, devices to counterbalance the Doppler effect have been constructed.

2.8.2 Mach-Zehnder Tunable Filters

If the length difference that determines which wavelength recombines at what output port of the Mach-Zehnder filter is controllable, then the filter can become tunable. This is accomplished by altering the refractive index of the path by the application of heat. A polymer material known to change its refractive index when exposed to heat is perfluoro-cyclobutane (PFCB).

The wavelength selectability of Mach-Zehnder filters constitutes them as tunable *optical frequency discriminators* (OFDs).

2.8.3 Birefringence Filters

The properties of birefringent crystals may be used to construct optical tunable filters. Consider two quarter-wave birefringent disks positioned in parallel and such that the first disk has its fast axis at $+45°$ and the second at $-45°$ (Figure 2.4).

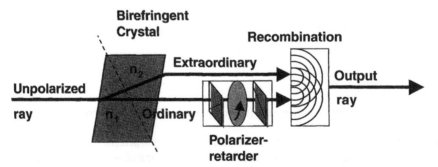

Figure 2.4 Principles of a birefringence filter; the incident beam is split in the ordinary and extraordinary rays; one propagates through a polarizer and retarder.

Based on this, the retardation to a monochromatic beam propagating in the z-axis is summed up to zero because one disk accelerates as much as the other decelerates. If one of the two disks is rotated by an angle $45° + \rho$, then an acceleration or a deceleration proportional to the angle ρ is introduced, and a phase-controlling mechanism is constructed. Now, if prior to entering the first disk a birefringent crystal splits the beam in two (the ordinary and extraordinary rays), then each ray is controlled differently than the other, and as they recombine at the output, a tuning mechanism or a tunable filter is constructed.

2.9 DIFFRACTION GRATINGS

A *diffraction grating* is an arrayed slit device that takes advantage of the diffraction property of light and reflects light in a direction that depends on the angle of incident light, the wavelength, and the grating constant (Figure 2.5). That is, a grating diffracts wavelengths in different directions when a mixed-wavelength beam impinges on it. The blaze angle and the number of slits per unit length characterize a diffraction grating.

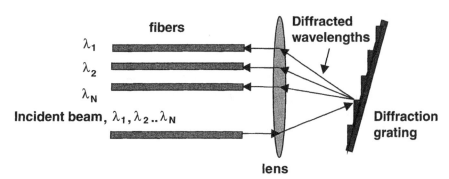

Figure 2.5 Each wavelength component of a collimated polychromatic light beam is diffracted and directed to a different point in space.

2.10 ARRAYED WAVEGUIDE GRATING

Arrayed waveguide gratings (AWGs) are filters of the Mach-Zehnder type. They can be monolithically manufactured to support many optical channels (SiO_2 AWGs for 128 channels and 25-GHz channel spacing as well as InP AWGs for 64 channels with 50-GHz channel spacing have been reported).

2.11   DIRECTIONAL COUPLERS

Optical directional couplers are solid-state devices that transfer the maximum possible optical power from one or more optical device(s) to another in a selected direction. Power transfer may be from a light source to a fiber, from fiber to fiber, from fiber to device (such as to a filter or a demultiplexer), and from device to fiber.

Single-mode fiber directional couplers use the evanescent property of integrated light guides on a substrate to couple optical power (light) of certain wavelength from one guide to another. When a voltage V is applied, optical power is guided through the same guide, however with a phase change. When the applied voltage $V = 0$, then power is transferred through the evanescent separation region to the adjacent guide.

For maximum power transfer, the proximity of two light guides, the synchronization of the two phase velocities, the refractive index, and the interaction (or coupling) length L_0 are important parameters in couplers.

When the isolation between the two light guides over the length L_0 is controlled, a controllable device may be made. Then, in addition to being a directional coupler, such a device may be used as a power attenuator, a signal modulator, power splitters, isolators, and an on-off switch.

2.12   OPTICAL ISOLATORS

Optical isolators are devices that transmit optical power (of a band of wavelengths) in one direction more than the other direction.

Optical isolator devices are characterized by *insertion loss L,* or the loss of optical power through it, and by *isolation I,* or the ratio of transmitted power in one direction over the other direction. Ideally, it should allow transmission of all power in one direction and no power in the other direction; that is, $L = 0$ and $I = \infty$.

2.13   POLARIZERS, ROTATORS, AND CIRCULATORS

Optical isolators are made with certain materials (formed in parallel plates or prisms) that allow one polarization direction of nonpolarized light to propagate through it. These devices are called *polarizers.* Birefringent materials can be used as polarizers.

Other materials rotate the polarization direction by an angle, and they are called *rotators.* Rotators are based on the Faraday effect. Rotators can be made with fibers doped with elements or compounds that have a large Verdet constant, such as terbium (Tb), yttrium-iron-garnet ($Y_3Fe_5O_{12}$ or YIG), and bismuth-substituted terbium-iron-garnet ($Tb_{3-x}Bi_xFe_5O_{12}$ or TbBiIG). Some of them may require a strong magnetic field, such as the YIGs.

Polarizers and rotators can be combined to form isolators. Isolators may be viewed as two-port devices that allow unidirectional energy to flow from one terminal to the other. Now, if a structure is made with more than one isolator, then a three-terminal device is constructed that permits unidirectional optical energy to flow from terminal 1 to 2, from 2 to 3, and from 3 to 1 but not in any other direction. This device is known as a *circulator* (Figure 2.6).

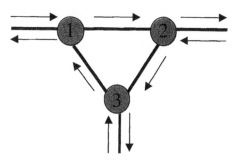

Figure 2.6 Principles of a circulator and its symbol.

2.14 OPTICAL EQUALIZERS

The wavelengths of a generated spectral range are not all of the same amplitude. However, for proper operation at the receiving end it is necessary to have a flat output power spectrum. Optical equalizers monitor each wavelength channel at the output and selectively make amplitude adjustments to flatten the optical power of the spectrum within a band of wavelengths.

The key desirable characteristics of optical equalizers are:

- Large wavelength range
- Low ripple of the spectrum amplitude (small peak-to-peak variation)
- High dynamic range
- Low loss
- Polarization independence
- Fast acquisition

2.15 SUPERPRISMS

When a collimated (parallel) beam of polychromatic light impinges on one of the prism surfaces (AB), then each frequency component is refracted differently.

The output light from the prism consists of the frequency components separated from each other by a small angle. However, this angle is very small, and to achieve good resolution of wavelengths, a substantial distance is required, thus making this impractical in many multiplexer/demultiplexer (Mux/Demux) applications. This is addresed with superprisms.

Superprisms are artificially made prisms the material of which forms a lattice known as *photonic crystalline*. Photonic crystalline optical material is an artificial structure with a periodic dielectric fabricated on Si. The periodicity of the crystalline lattice is three dimensional and using nanotechnology is several tens of nanometers (reported at 180 nm). Photonic crystalline structures act as highly disperssive structures that exhibit much superior angular dispersion characteristics (reported at 500 times higher) than conventional prisms (hence superprisms).

2.16 OPTICAL MULTIPLEXERS AND DEMULTIPLEXERS

The main function of an optical multiplexer is to couple two or more wavelengths into the same fiber. In general, optical multiplexers consist of a multiplicity of input fibers, each carrying an optical signal at different wavelength.

The demultiplexer undoes what the multiplexer has done; it separates a multiplicity of wavelengths in a fiber and directs them to many fibers. Most optical passive demultiplexers, such as prisms and gratings, may also be used as optical multiplexers.

2.17 OPTICAL CROSS-CONNECTS

Optical cross-connect devices are modeled after the many-port model. That is, N input ports and N output ports, and a table that defines the connectivity between input and one or more outputs.

All-optical cross-connect fabrics are based on at least three methods:

1. Free-space optical switching [waveguide grating routers (WGR) Mach-Zehnder interferometers]
2. Optical solid-state devices (acousto-optic and electro-optic couplers)
3. Electromechanical mirror-based devices

Other cross-connect fabrics are based on the polarization properties of liquid crystals and other properties of materials. Optical switches based on liquid crystal technology are relatively of limited size, up to 40 channels, but they offer high isolation, low insertion loss, and low cost.

2.17.1 Free-Space Optical Switching

Among the most promising switches with many input ports to many output ports are the generalized Mach-Zehnder WGRs. In this device, a given wavelength at any input port appears at a specified output port (Figure 2.7). Thus, an input-to-output connectivity map is constructed, that is, a switch. This type of free-space optical switching is also known as *wavelength routing*.

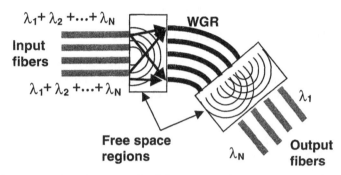

Figure 2.7 A waveguide grating router (WRG) is a generalized Mach-Zehnder interferometer.

2.17.2 Solid-State Cross-Connects

Solid-state optical cross-connect devices are 2×2 semiconductor directional couplers, taking advantage of the controllable index of refraction of ferroelectric LiNbO3 crystals by the application of an external electric field. Several 2×2 switches can be monolithically integrated to produce a larger switch. Although the number of ports can be large (e.g., 128×128), due to cumulative losses, practical switches have a rather limited number of ports (e.g., 16×16 and perhaps 32×32).

The material type, the controlling mechanism, and the controlled property impact the switching speed of the device as well as the number of ports of the switch. For example, switches made with $LiNbO_3$ crystals exhibit switching speeds on the order of nanoseconds whereas those made with SiO_2 on Si exhibit speeds on the order of under 1 ms.

Solid-state optical cross-connecting devices are characterized by a number of parameters:

- Size of switching matrix (e.g., 2×2, 4×4)
- Insertion loss (typically 1 dB)
- Isolation (typically 35 dB)
- Cross-talk (typically -40 dB)

- Switching speed (in the range milliseconds to nanoseconds)
- Polarization-dependent loss (fraction of a decibel)
- Spectral flatness (typically ±1 dB)
- Operating temperature (0–70°C)
- Operating voltage (typically +5 V)
- Number of inputs and outputs (e.g., 2 inputs, 2 outputs in a 2 × 2)
- Blocking or nonblocking switching fabrics

2.17.3 Micro-Electromechanical Switches

A technology known as nanotechnology has been employed to micromachine many tiny mirrors on the same substrate. An actual microphotograph of this technology, known as a micro-electromechanical system (MEMS), is shown Figure 2.8.

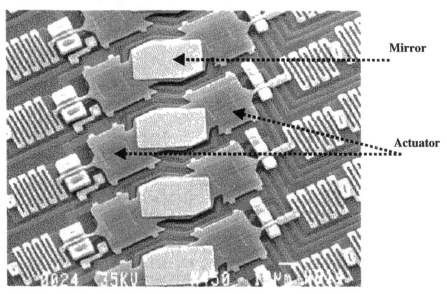

Figure 2.8 Array of micromachined mirrors, magnified 450 times. (Copyright © 1999 by Lucent Technologies. Reprinted with permission.)

When a beam impinges on one of the mirrors, by reflecting the beam accordingly, the beam may be directed to one of many outputs, thus constructing an optical switch (Figure 2.9).

The MEMS technology enables the integration of an $N \times N$ mirror matrix, where N can be potentially higher than 1000. However, the precision of tilting the mirrors and the time required to tilt a large quantity of them at their desirable position are very critical. Minor deviations in angle position may increase optical sig-

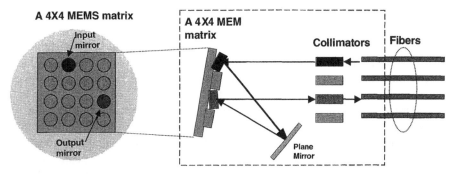

Figure 2.9 MEMS in a matrix configuration comprising an $n \times n$ connectivity matrix.

nal loss (due to beam misalignment) and increase cross-talk. Moreover, as a mirror changes position, the reflected light beam traverses the optical field of other output fibers. Therefore, caution should be taken so that the reflected beam is not coupled to these traversed output fibers and thus contribute to bit error rate. Current designs have minimized the coupled optical power in traversed output fibers.

2.17.4 Switching Speeds

Currently, the speed of optical switching devices depends on the materials used to make the switch, the principle on which the switch operates, and the technology. Although speed is an important parameter, there are many more parameters that one should consider in the selection of the switch type, such as optical loss, dispersion, reliability, stability, switching-matrix size, external voltages (if any), temperature dependence, physical size, and cost. Switching speeds vary from seconds to nanoseconds:

Technology	Switching Speed
Thermo-optic switching	ms
Acousto-optic switching	ms
Electro-optic ceramic-compound switching	μs
MEMS switching	μs
SiO_2 on Si planar	ms–μs
$LiNbO_3$ switching	ns
Nonlinear electro-optic polymer APII devices (amino-phenylene-isophorone-isoxazolone)	ps (in experimental phase)

2.18   OPTICAL ADD-DROP MULTIPLEXERS

The *optical add-drop multiplexer* (OADM) is a DWDM function. It selectively removes (drops) a wavelength from a multiplicity of wavelengths in a fiber and thus removes traffic on this channel. Then, in the same direction of data flow it adds the same wavelength but with different data content.

OADMs are classified in *fixed* wavelength and in *dynamically* wavelength selectable OADMs. Figure 2.10 illustrates an OADM with a 2 × 2 $LiNbO_3$ or an array of micromirrors, and Figure 2.11 an OADM with a grating. Other technologies may also be used. The type of technology deployed in an OADM depends on the number of wavelengths in WDM, the number of wavelengths dropped and added (typically one or very few), the network level (e.g., access, metro, transport short haul or long haul), and cost.

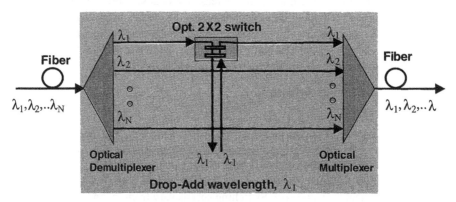

Figure 2.10 Principles of an optical drop-first/then-add multiplexer using an optical 2 × 2 switch.

2.19   OPTICAL AMPLIFIERS

Optical amplifiers (OAs) are key devices that reconstitute the attenuated optical signal and thus expand the effective fiber span between two points, the data source and the destination.

Optical amplifiers are devices based on conventional laser principles. They receive one or more optical signals, each at a center frequency, and simultaneously they amplify all wavelengths. This, as compared with regenerators, is a significant advantage in multiwavelength (WDM) fiber systems, since one device replaces many.

There are two types of OAs, the semiconductor laser-type optical amplifiers (SOA) and the doped fiber-type amplifier (EDFA for doped with erbium and PDFA for doped with praseodymium).

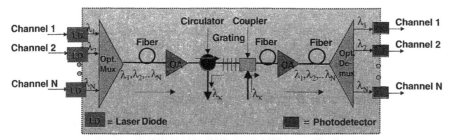

Figure 2.11 Principles of an optical drop-first/then-add multiplexer using a fiber grating.

There are also other amplifying devices that depend on the nonlinear properties of optical materials, such as the Raman.

Optical amplifiers require electrical or optical energy to excite (pump up) the state of electron-hole pairs. Energy is typically provided by injecting electrical current (in SOA) or optical light in the ultraviolet (UV) range (in EDFA).

Amplifiers are characterized by gain, bandwidth, gain over the bandwidth, maximum output power, dynamic range, cross-talk, noise figure, output saturation power, and physical size. The output saturation power is defined as the output power level at which the amplifier's gain has dropped by 3 dB.

Some key characteristics of optical amplifiers are gain, gain efficiency, gain bandwidth, gain saturation, noise, and polarization sensitivity:

- *Gain* is the ratio of output power to input power (measured in decibels).

- *Gain efficiency* is the gain as a function of input power (decibels per milliwatt).

- Bandwidth is a function of frequency, and as such *gain bandwidth* is the range of frequencies over which the amplifier is effective.

- *Gain saturation* is the maximum output power of the amplifier, beyond which it cannot increase despite the input power increase.

- *Noise* is an inherent characteristic of amplifiers. In optical amplifiers, noise is due to spontaneous light emission of excited ions.

- *Polarization sensitivity* is the gain dependence of optical amplifiers on the polarization of the signal.

In optical communications networks, there are two distinct amplification methods: the *regenerator* and the *optical amplifier.*

2.19.1 SOAs

The most important advantage of SOAs is that they are made with InGaAsP and thus are small and compact and may be integrated with other semiconductor and optical components. However, in contrast to EDFAs, SOAs have a high noise figure (more than 6 dB over 50 nm) and a high cross-talk level due to nonlinear phenomena (four-wave mixing). Nevertheless, SOAs are solid-state compact devices that can also be used as wavelength converters and regenerators and in optical signal processing applications.

2.19.2 Rare-Earth Doped Fiber Amplifiers

Fiber-optic amplifiers (FOAs) in DWDM systems are heavily doped with rare-earth elements. The attractiveness of rare-earth elements is that they fluoresce in the spectrum of minimum loss (or absorption) of conventional silica fiber. For example, Nd^{3+} and Er^{3+} emit in the range of 1.3 and 1.5 μm, respectively.

Based on this, one of the most successful doped fibers is the EDFA. The erbium ions may be excited by a number of optical frequencies: 514, 532, 667, 800, 980, and 1480 nm. These frequencies excite erbium ions to higher energy levels from where they drop to one of four intermediate metastable levels radiating phonons (the acoustical quantum equivalent of a photon).

Those in the lowest metastable level finally drop spontaneously after about 10 ms (known as *spontaneous lifetime*) to the initial (ground) level, emitting photons at a wavelength in the range of 1550 nm (i.e., the C-band), unless a photon (in the 1550-nm range) passes by to stimulate photon emission. The spontaneous lifetime adds to the noise content of the optical signal, known as amplifier spontaneous emission (ASE).

An EDFA amplifier consists of one or two excitation lasers (known as the *pump*), a coupling device, an erbium-doped fiber, and two isolators, one isolator per EDFA end. The two most convenient excitation wavelengths are 980 and 1480 nm at an output optical power from under 100 mW to about 250 mW. Pump lasers are specifically designed for EDFA applications.

PDFAs have a high gain (~30 dB) and a high saturation power (20 dBm) and are suitable in the region 1280–1340 nm that EDFAs are not. However, PDFAs require a nonsilica fiber (fluoride) that is not very common, and they require a high-power (up to 300-mW) pump laser at 1017 nm (not the popular 980 or 1480 nm). An alternative to this is fibers that contain elements such as gallium and lanthanum (gallium-lanthanum-sulfide and gallium-lanthanum-iodine).

Designing with EDFAs, several issues should be addressed:

1. The first issue is flat gain. EDFAs do not amplify all wavelengths through them the same; thus, the gain is not exactly flat.
2. The second issue is pump power sharing. The pump power is shared by all wavelengths. Thus, the more wavelengths, the less power per wavelength. However, as wavelengths may be dropped and not added, or some wavelengths are lost due to failures, EDFAs amplify fewer wavelengths more.

These two issues are addressed by properly engineering the WDM system and by dynamic gain control.

3. The third issue is not as simple and is addressed differently. When engineering a fiber-optic path, it should be remembered that optical noise sources are cumulative and that the ASE of EDFAs introduces noise that degrades the signal to noise ratio (S/N). Although a strong optical signal launched into the fiber could overcome this, near the zero-dispersion wavelength region four-wave mixing would become dominant and it would degrade the S/N ratio.

2.19.3 Raman Amplifiers

Raman amplifiers are nondoped fiber amplifiers that employ high-power pump lasers to take advantage of the nonlinearity stimulated Raman scattering (SRS) properties of the fiber. Raman amplifiers have their pump near the receiver and the pump light travels in the opposite direction toward the source. Thus, the pump is strongest at the receiver and weakest at the source. This has an important advantage, the pump power is found where mostly needed (at remote distances from the source) and less needed (in the vicinity of the source). Consequently, the signal is amplified where it is the weakest and less where it is the strongest. In addition, four-wave mixing effects are thus minimized.

In a different configuration, there may be two pumps, one at the transmitting side and one at the receiving side, with each pump at different wavelengths (to achieve simultaneous C- and L-band amplification). However, this arrangement is still experimental, and certain nonlinearity issues (FWM, polarization), signal-pump interactions, increased optical signal-to-noise ratio (OSNR), and Rayleigh reflection (which may induce a lasing effect) need to be resolved.

The most important feature of Raman amplifiers is that they are nonresonant and have a wide bandwidth range that can extend over the complete useful spectrum from 1300 to 1600+ nm (i.e., 500 optical channels at 100-GHz spacing) with no restriction to gain bandwidth. This enables a multi-terabit transmission technology, also referred to as *Raman supercontinuum.* On the negative side, Raman amplifiers require very long fibers (on the order of several kilometers) and pump lasers with high optical power (~1 W), and thus thermal management issues as well as safety issues become nontrivial.

2.20 CLASSIFICATION OF OPTICAL FIBER AMPLIFIERS

The OFAs are classified, similar to electronic and wireless systems, as power amplifiers, preamplifiers, and line amplifiers:

- A *power amplifier* is capable of increasing the optical power of the modulated photonic signal at the source. It is placed right after the source, and thus it may be integrated with it. It receives a large signal (from the laser source) with a large signal-to-noise ratio and it boosts its power to levels about -10 dBm or higher.

- A *preamplifier* is characterized by very low noise and large gain to increase a highly attenuated signal to a level that can be detected reliably by an optical detector. A preamplifier is placed directly before the detector and may be integrated with it.

- A *line amplifier* is characterized by large gain and low noise to amplify an already attenuated signal so that it can travel an additional length of fiber.

The significance of these classifications impacts the pump power level and overall cost of application of the amplifier as well as safety.

2.21 WAVELENGTH CONVERTERS

Wavelength conversion enables optical channels to be relocated, adding to the flexibility and efficiency of multiwavelength systems. Wavelength conversion may be achieved by employing the nonlinearity properties of certain heterojunction semiconductors.

Semiconductor optical amplifiers (SOAs) are also used as wavelength-converting devices. Their basic structure consists of an active layer (erbium-doped waveguide) sandwiched between a *p*-layer InP and an *n*-layer InP.

Currently, various methods have been explored based on *cross-gain modulation, four-wave mixing, dispersion-shifted fiber,* and other *interferometric* techniques.

REFERENCES

[1] S. V. Kartalopoulos, *Introduction to DWDM Technology: Data in a Rainbow,* IEEE Press, New York, 2000.

[2] C. A. Brackett, "Dense Wavelength Division Multiplexing Networks: Principles and Applications," *IEEE JSAC,* vol. 8, no. 6, 1990, pp. 948–964.

[3] K. Nosu, *Optical FDM Network Technologies,* Artech House, Boston, 1997.

[4] R. G. Hunsperger, Ed., *Photonic Devices and Systems,* Marcel Dekker, New York, 1994.

[5] R. G. Hunsperger, *Integrated Optics: Theory and Technology,* Springer-Verlag, New York, 1984.

[6] H. Toba and K. Nosu, "Optical Frequency Division Multiplexing System-Review of Key Technologies and Applications," *IEICE Trans. Commun.,* vol. E75-B, no. 4, 1992, pp. 243–255.

[7] S. V. Kartalopoulos, *Understanding SONET/SDH and ATM: Communications Networks for the Next Millennium,* IEEE Press, New York, 1999.

[8] L. Desmarais, *Applied Electro-Optics,* Prentice-Hall, Englewood Cliffs, NJ, 1999.

[9] B. Mukherjee, *Optical Communication Networks,* McGraw-Hill, New York, 1997.

[10] J. C. Palais, *Fiber Optic Communications,* 3rd ed., Prentice-Hall, Englewood Cliffs, NJ, 1992.

[11] R. Ramaswami and K. N. Sivarajan, *Optical Networks,* Morgan Kaufmann, San Francisco, CA, 1998.

[12] M. H. Freeman, *Optics,* 10th ed., Butterworths, London, 1990.

[13] K. Nassau, *The Physics and Chemistry of Color,* Wiley, New York, 1983.

[14] T. Wildi, *Units and Conversion Charts,* 2nd ed., IEEE Press, New York, 1995.

[15] A. J. Lowery, "Computer-Aided Photonics Design," *IEEE Spectrum,* vol. 34, no. 4, 1997, pp. 26–31.

[16] M. Cvijetic, *Coherent and Nonlinear Lightwave Communications,* Artech House, Boston, 1996.

[17] P. S. Henry, "Lightwave Primer," *IEEE J. Quant. Electron.,* vol. QE-21, 1985, pp. 1862–1879.

[18] R. Marz, *Integrated Optics: Design and Modeling,* Artech House, Boston, 1995.

[19] J. Hecht, *Understanding Fiber Optics,* Prentice-Hall, Englewood Cliffs, NJ, 1999.

[20] S. V. Kartalopoulos, "A Plateau of Performance?" Guest Editorial, *IEEE Commun. Mag.,* Sept. 1992, pp. 13–14.

[21] J. Nellist, *Understanding Telecommunications and Lightwave Systems,* IEEE Press, New York, 1996.

[22] R. Driggers, P. Cox, and T. Edwards, *An Introduction to Infrared and Electro-Optical Systems,* Artech House, Boston, 1999.

[23] L. G. Kazovsky, "Optical Signal Processing for Lightwave Communications Networks," *IEEE JSAC,* vol. 8, no. 6, 1990, pp. 973–982.

[24] N. Shibata, K. Nosu, K. Iwashita, and Y. Azuma, "Transmission Limitations Due to Fiber Nonlinearities in Optical FDM Systems," *IEEE J. Selected Areas Commun.,* vol. 8, no. 6. 1990, pp. 1068–1077.

[25] S. E. Miller, "Coupled-Wave Theory and Waveguide Applications," *Bell Syst. Tech. J.,* vol. 33, 1954, pp. 661–719.

[26] A. Yariv, "Coupled Mode Theory for Guided Wave Optics," *IEEE J. Quant. Electron.,* vol QE-9, 1973, pp. 919–933.

[27] T. K. Findakly, "Glass Waveguides by Ion Exchange: A Review," *Opt. Eng.,* vol. 24, 1985, pp. 244–255.

[28] J. R. Thompson and R. Roy, "Multiple Four-Wave Mixing Process in an Optical Fiber," *Opt. Lett.,* vol. 16, no. 8, 1991, pp. 557–559.

[29] K. Inoue, "Experimental Study on Channel Crosstalk Due to Fiber Four-Wave Mixing Around the Zero-Dispersion Wavelength," *IEEE J. Lighwave Technol.,* vol. LT-12, no. 6, 1994, pp. 1023–1028.

[30] K. Inoue, "Suppression of Fiber Four-Wave Mixing in Multichannel Transmission Using Birefringent Elements," *IEICE Trans. Commun.,* vol. E76-B, no. 9, 1993, pp. 1219–1221.

[31] K. Inoue, "Four-Wave Mixing in an Optical Fiber in the Zero-Dispersion Wavelength Region," *IEEE J. Lighwave Technol.,* vol. LT-10, no. 11, 1992, pp. 1553–1563.

[32] N. Shibata, K. Nosu, K. Iwashita, and Y. Azuma, "Transmission Limitations Due to Fiber Nonlinearities in Optical FDM Systems," *IEEE J. Selected Areas Commun.,* vol. 8, no. 6. 1990, pp. 1068–1077.

[33] J. Hecht, *The Laser Guidebook,* 2nd ed., Tab Books, Blue Ridge Summit, PA, 1992.

[34] J. LaCourse, "Laser Primer for Fiber-Optics Users," *IEEE Circuits Devices Mag.,* vol. 8, no. 2, 1992, pp. 27–32.

[35] M. Zirngibl, "Multifrequency Lasers and Applications in WDM Networks," *IEEE Commun. Mag.,* vol. 36, no. 12, 1998, pp. 39–41.

[36] U. Koren et al., "Wavelength Division Multiplexing Light Sources with Integrated Quantum Well Tunable Lasers and Optical Amplification," *Appl. Phys. Lett.,* vol. 54, 1989, pp. 2056–2058.

[37] M. J. Adams, "Theory of Twin-Guide Fabry-Perot Laser Amplifiers," *IEE Proc.,* vol. 136, no. 5, 1989, pp. 287–292.

[38] K. S. Giboney, L. A. Aronson, and B. E. Lemoff, "The Ideal Light Source for Datanets," *IEEE Spectrum,* vol. 35, no. 2, 1998, pp. 43–53.

[39] K. Kobayashi and I. Mito, "Single Frequency and Tunable Laser Diodes," *J. Lightwave Technol.,* vol 6. 1988, pp. 1623–1633.

[40] M-C. Amann and W. Thulke, "Continuously Tunable Laser Diodes: Longitudinal versus Transverse Tuning Scheme," *IEEE JSAC,* vol. 8, no. 6, 1990, pp. 1169–1177.

[41] L. A. Coldren and S. W. Corzine, "Continuously Tunable Single Frequency Semiconductor Lasers," *IEEE J. Quant. Electron.,* vol. QE-23, 1987, pp. 903–908.

[42] M. Okuda and K. Onaka, "Tunability of Distributed Bragg Reflector Laser by Modulating Refractive Index in Corrugated Waveguide," *Jpn. J. Appl. Phys.,* vol. 16, 1977, pp. 1501–1502.

[43] Y. Kotaki, M. Matsuda, H. Ishikawa, and H. Imai, "Tunable DBR Laser with Wide Tuning Range," *Electron. Lett.,* vol. 24, 1988, pp. 503–505.

[44] S. Adachi, "Refractive Indices of III–IV Compounds: Key Properties of InGaAsP Relevant to Device Design," *J. Appl. Phys.,* vol. 53, 1982, pp. 5863–5869.

[45] J. G. Eden, "Photochemical Processing of Semiconductors: New Applications for Visible and Ultraviolet Lasers," *IEEE Circuits Devices Mag.,* vol. 2, no. 1, 1986, pp. 18–24.

[46] A. Yariv, "Quantum Well Semiconductor Lasers Are Taking Over," *IEEE Circuits Devices Mag.,* vol. 5, no. 6, 1989, pp. 25–28.

[47] J. LaCourse, "Laser Primer for Fiber-Optics Users," *IEEE Circuits Devices Mag.,* vol. 8, no. 2, 1992, pp. 27–32.

[48] D. Botez and L. J. Mawst, "Phase-Locked Laser Arrays Revisited," *IEEE Circuits Devices Mag.,* vol. 12, no. 11, 1996, pp. 25–32.

[49] Z. V. Nesterova and I. V. Aleksaandrov, "Optical-Fiber Sources of Coherent Light," *Sov. J. Opt. Technol.,* vol 54, no. 3, 1987, pp. 183–190.

[50] N. K. Dutta, "III–V Device Technologies for Lightwave Applications," *AT&T Tech. J.,* vol. 68, no. 1, 1989, pp. 5–18.

[51] G. Coquin, K. W. Cheung, and M. Choy, "Single- and Multiple-Wavelength Operation of Acousto-Optically Tuned Lasers at 1.3 Microns," *Proc. 11th IEEE Int. Semiconductor Laser Conf.*, Boston, 1988, pp. 130–131.

[52] R. C. Alferness, "Waveguide Electro-Optic Modulators," *IEEE Trans. Microwave Theory Techn.*, vol. MTT-30, 1982, pp. 1121–1137.

[53] D. Nesset, T. Kelly, and D. Marcenac, "All-Optical Wavelength Conversion Using SOA Nonlinearities," *IEEE Commun. Mag.*, vol. 36, no. 12, 1998, pp. 56–61.

[54] S. D. Personick, "Receiver Design for Digital Fiber Optic Communication Systems, I," *Bell Syst. Tech. J.*, vol. 52, no. 6, 1973, pp. 843–874.

[55] S. D. Personick, "Receiver Design for Digital Fiber Optic Communication Systems, II," *Bell Syst. Tech. J.*, vol. 52, no. 6, 1973, pp. 875–886.

[56] F. Tong, "Multiwavelength Receivers for WDM Systems," *IEEE Commun. Mag.*, vol. 36, no. 12, 1998, pp. 42–49.

[57] K. Inoue, "Experimental Study on Channel Crosstalk Due to Fiber Four-Wave Mixing around the Zero-Dispersion Wavelength," *IEEE J. Lighwave Technol.*, vol. LT-12, no. 6, 1994, pp. 1023–1028.

[58] K.-W. Cheung, "Acoustooptic Tunable Filters in Narrowband WDM Networks: System Issues and Network Applications," *IEEE JSAC*, vol. 8, no. 6, 1990, pp. 1015–1025.

[59] D. A. Smith, J. E. Baran, J. J. Johnson, and K.-W. Cheung, "Integrated-Optic Acoustically-Tunable Filters for WDM Networks," *IEEE JSAC*, vol. 8, no. 6, 1990, pp. 1151–1159.

[60] S. R. Mallison, "Wavelength-Selective Filters for Single-Mode Fiber WDM Systems Using Fabry-Perot Interferometers," *Appl. Opt.*, vol 26, 1987, pp. 430–436.

[61] N. Takato et al., "Silica-Based Integrated Optic Mach-Zehnder Multi/Demultiplexer Family with Channel Spacing of 0.01–250 nm," *IEEE JSAC*, vol. 8, no. 6, 1990, pp. 1120–1127.

[62] W. Warzanskyj, F. Heisman, and R. C. Alferness, "Polarization-Independent Electro-Acoustically Tunable Narrow-Band Wavelength Filter," *Appl. Phys. Lett.*, vol. 56, 1990, pp. 2009–2011.

[63] J. Frangen et al., "Integrated Optical, Acoustically-Tunable Wavelength Filter," *Proc. 6th European Conf. Integrated Opt.*, Paris, SPIE, 1989, post-deadline paper.

[64] F. Heismann, L. Buhl, and R. C. Alferness, "Electrooptically Tunable Narrowband Ti:LiNbO3 Wavelength Filter," *Electron. Lett.*, vol. 23, 1987, pp. 572–573.

[65] N. Goto and Y. Miyazaki, "Integrated Optical Multi-/Demultiplexer Using Acoustooptic Effect for Multiwavelength Optical Communications," *IEEE JSAC*, vol. 8, no. 6, 1990, pp. 1160–1168.

[66] R. M. Measures, A. T. Alavie, M. LeBlanc, S. Huang, M. Ohn, R. Masskant, and D. Graham, "Controlled Grating Chirp for Variable Optical Dispersion Compensation," *Proceedings, 13th Annual Conference on European Fiber Optic Communications and Networks*, Brighton, England, 1995, pp. 38–41.

[67] G. D. Boyd and F. Heismann, "Tunable Acoustooptic Reflection Filters in LiNbO3 without a Doppler Shift," *J. Lightwave Technol.*, vol. 7, 1989, pp. 625–631.

[68] D. Sadot and E. Boimovich, "Tunable Optical Filters for Dense WDM Networks," *IEEE Commun. Mag.*, vol. 36, no. 12, 1998, pp. 50–55.

[69] H. Kobrinski and K. W. Cheung, "Wavelength-Tunable Optical Filters: Applications and Technologies," *IEEE Commun. Mag.*, vol. 27, 1989, pp. 53–63.

[70] C. M. Ragdale, D. Reid, D. J. Robbins, and J. Buus, "Narrowband Fiber Grating Filters," *IEEE JSAC*, vol. 8, no. 6, 1990, pp. 1146–1150.

[71] J. Stone and D. Marcuse, "Ultrahigh Finesse Fiber Fabry-Perot Interferometers," *J. Lightwave Technol.*, vol. LT-4, no. 4, 1986, pp. 382–385.

[72] A. A. M. Saleh and J. Stone, "Two-Stage Fabry-Perot Filters as Demultiplexers in Optical FDMA LAN's," *J. Lightwave Technol.*, vol. LT-7, 1989, pp. 323–330.

[73] S. R. Mallinson, "Wavelength Selective Filters for Single-Mode Fiber WDM Systems Using Fabry-Perot Interferometers," *Appl. Opt.*, vol. 26, 1987, pp. 430–436.

[74] G. Hernandez, *Fabry-Perot Interferometers*, Cambridge University Press, Cambridge, 1986.

[75] F. J. Leonberger, "Applications of Guided-Wave Interferometers," *Laser Focus*, 1982, pp. 125–129.

[76] H. Van de Stadt and J. M. Muller, "Multimirror Fabry-Perot Interferometers," *J. Opt. Soc. Am. A*, vol. 2, 1985, pp. 1363–1370.

[77] P. A. Humblet and W. M. Hamdy, "Crosstalk Analysis and Filter Optimization of Single- and Double-Cavity Fabry-Perot Filters," *IEEE JSAC*, vol. 8, no. 6, 1990, pp. 1095–1107.

[78] H. Takahashi et al., "Arrayed-Waveguide Grating for Wavelength Division Multiplexing/Demultiplexing with Nanometer Resolution," *Electron. Lett.*, vol. 26, 1990, pp. 87–88.

[79] J. Minowa and Y. Fujii, "Dielectric Multilayer Thin Film Filters for WDM Transmission," *IEEE J. Lightwave Technol.*, vol. 1, no. 1, 1983, pp. 116–121.

[80] W. K. Chen, *Passive and Active Filters*, Wiley, New York, 1986.

[81] H. Kobrinski and K-W. Cheung, "Wavelength-Tunable Optical Filters: Applications and Technologies," *IEEE Commun. Mag.*, Oct. 1989, pp. 53–63.

[82] S. Kawakami, "Light Propagation along Periodic Metal-Dielectric Layers," *Appl. Opt.*, vol. 22, 1983, p. 2426.

[83] J. W. Evans, "The Birefringent Filter," *J. Opt. Soc. Am.*, vol. 39, 1949, p. 229.

[84] H. Van de Stadt and J. M. Muller, "Multimirror Fabry-Perot Interferometers", *J. Opt. Soc. Am. A*, vol. 2, 1985, pp. 1363–1370.

[85] R. J. von Gutfeld, "Laser-Enhanced Plating and Etching for Microelectronic Applications," *IEEE Circuits Devices Mag.*, vol. 2, no. 1, 1986, pp. 57–60.

[86] J. Bokor, A. R. Neureuther, and W. G. Oldham, "Advanced Lithography for ULSI," *IEEE Circuits Devices Mag.*, vol. 12, no. 1, 1996, pp. 11–15.

[87] J. J. Refi, "Optical Fibers for Optical Networking," *Bell Labs Tech. J.*, vol. 4, no. 1, 1999, pp. 246–261.

[88] W. D. Johnston, Jr., M. A. DiGiuseppe, and D. P. Wilt, "Liquid and Vapor Phase Growth of III–V Materials for Photonic Devices," *AT&T Tech. J.*, vol. 68, no. 1, 1989, pp. 53–63.

[89] W. G. Dautremont-Smith, R. J. McCoy, and R. H. Burton, "Fabrication Technologies for III–V Compound Semiconductor Photonic and Electronic Devices," *AT&T Tech. J.*, vol. 68, no. 1, 1989, pp. 64–82.

[90] N. K. Dutta, "III–V Device Technologies for Lightwave Applications," *AT&T Tech. J.*, vol. 68, no. 1, 1989, pp. 5–18.

[91] S. Adachi, "Refractive Indices of III–IV Compounds: Key Properties of InGaAsP Relevant to Device Design," *J. Appl. Phys.*, vol. 53, 1982, pp. 5863–5869.

[92] T. Komukai, et al., "Upconversion Pumped Thulium-Doped Fluoride Fiber Amplifier and Laser Operating at 1.47 μm," *IEEE Quant. Electron.*, vol. 31, 1995, pp. 1880–1889.

[93] R. Driggers, P. Cox, and T. Edwards, *An Introduction to Infrared and Electro-Optical Systems*, Artech House, Boston, 1999.

[94] G. Eisenstein, "Semiconductor Optical Amplifiers," *IEEE Circuits Devices Mag.*, vol. 5, no. 4, 1989, pp. 25–30.

[95] D. Nesset, T. Kelly, and D. Marcenac, "All-Optical Wavelength Conversion Using SOA Nonlinearities," *IEEE Commun. Mag.*, vol. 36, no. 12, 1998, pp. 56–61.

[96] S. Sudo, Ed., *Optical Fiber Amplifiers: Materials, Devices, and Applications*, Artech House, Boston, 1997.

[97] R. J. Mears, L. Reekie, I. M. Jauncey, and D. N. Payne, "Low-Noise Erbium-Doped Fiber Amplifier Operating at 1.54 μm," *Electron. Lett.*, vol. 23, no. 19, 1987, pp. 1026–1028.

[98] E. Desurvire, J. R. Simpson, and P. C. Becker, "High-Gain Erbium-Doped Traveling-Wave Fiber Amplifiers," *Opt. Lett.*, vol. 12, no. 11, 1987, pp. 888–890.

[99] Y. Sun, A. K. Srivastava, J. Zhou, and J. W. Sulhoff, "Optical Fiber Amplifiers for WDM Optical Networks," *Bell Labs Tech. J.*, vol. 4, no. 1, 1999, pp. 187–206.

[100] O. Ishida and H. Toba, "A 1.55-mm Lightwave Frequency Synthesizer," *IEICE Trans. Commun.*, vol. E75-B, no. 4, 1992, pp. 275–280.

[101] K. Vilhelmsson, "Simultaneous Forward and Backward Raman Scattering in Low-Attenuation Single-Mode Fibers," *J. Lightwave Technol.*, vol. LT-4, no. 4, 1986, pp. 400–404.

[102] J. G. Eden, "Photochemical Processing of Semiconductors: New Applications for Visible and Ultraviolet Lasers," *IEEE Circuits Devices Mag.*, vol. 2, no. 1, 1986, pp. 18–24.

[103] N. A. Olsson and J. Hegarty, "Noise Properties of a Raman Amplifier," *IEEE J. Lightwave Technol.*, vol. LT-4, no. 4, 1986, pp. 396–399.

[104] R. C. Alferness and L. L. Buhl, "Low-Cross-Talk Waveguide Polarization Multiplexer/Demultiplexer for λ = 1.32 μm," *Opt. Lett.*, vol 10, 1984, pp. 140–142.

[105] T. Hosaka, K. Okamoto, and J. Noda, "Single-Mode Fiber Type Polarizer," *IEEE J. Quant. Electron.*, vol. QE-18, 1982, p. 1569.

[106] R. A. Bergh, H. C. Lefevre, and H. J. Shaw, "Single-Mode Fiber-Optic Polarizer," *Opt. Lett.*, vol. 5, 1980, p. 479.

[107] W. Eickhoff, "In-Line Fiber-Optic Polarizer," *Electron. Lett.*, vol. 6, 1980, p. 762.

[108] R. C. Alferness and L. L. Buhl, "Low-Cross-Talk Waveguide Polarization Multiplexer/Demultiplexer for λ = 1.32 μm," *Opt. Lett.*, vol. 10, 1984, pp. 140–142.

[109] W. Warzanskyj, F. Heisman, and R. C. Alferness, "Polarization-Independent Electro-Acoustically Tunable Narrow-Band Wavelength Filter," *Appl. Phys. Lett.*, vol. 56, 1990, pp. 2009–2011.

[110] K. Shiraishi, S. Sugayama, and S. Kawakami, "Fiber Faraday Rotator," *Appl. Opt.,* vol. 23, 1984, p. 1103.

[111] S. E. Miller, "Coupled-Wave Theory and Waveguide Applications" *Bell Syst. Tech. J.,* vol. 33, 1954, pp. 661–719.

[112] A. Yariv, "Coupled Mode Theory for Guided Wave Optics," *IEEE J. Quant. Electron.,* vol QE-9, 1973, pp. 919–933.

[113] S-Y Lin and J. G. Fleming, "A Three-Dimensional Optical Photonic Crystal," *J. Lightwave Technol.,* Vol. 17, no. 11, 1999, pp. 1944–1947.

[114] H. Kosaka et al., "Superprism Phenomena in Photonic Crystals: Toward Microscale Lightwave Circuits," *J. Lightwave Technol.,* vol. 17, no. 11, 1999, pp. 2032–2038.

[115] U. Koren et al., "Wavelength Division Multiplexing Light Sources with Integrated Quantum Well Tunable Lasers and Optical Amplification," *Appl. Phys. Lett.,* vol. 54, 1989, pp. 2056–2058.

[116] G. J. Cannell. A. Robertson, and R. Worthington, "Practical Realization of a High Density Diode-Coupled Wavelength Demultiplexer," *IEEE JSAC,* vol. 8, no. 6, 1990, pp. 1141–1145.

[117] J. M. Senior and S. D. Cusworth, "Devices for Wavelength Multiplexing and Demultiplexing," *IEE Proc.,* vol. 136, no. 3, 1989, pp. 183–202.

[118] K. A. McGreer, "Arrayed Waveguide Grating for Wavelength Routing," *IEEE Commun. Mag.,* vol. 36, no. 12, 1998, pp. 62–68.

[119] M. K. Smit and C. van Dam, "PHASAR-Based WDM-Devices: Principles, Design and Application," *IEEE J. Sel. Topics Quant. Electron.,* vol. 2, no. 2, 1996, pp. 236–250.

[120] H. Tanobe et al., "Temperature Insensitive Arrayed Waveguide Gratings on InP Substrate," *IEEE Photon Tech. Lett.,* vol. 10, no. 2, 1998, pp. 235–237.

[121] T. Morioka and M. Saruwatari, "Ultrafast All-Optical Switching Utilizing the Optical Kerr Effect in Polarization Maintaining Single-Mode Fibers," *IEEE JSAC,* vol. 6, no. 7, 1988, pp. 1186–1198.

[122] A. Iocco, H. G. Limberger, and R. P. Salathe, "Bragg Grating Fast Tunable Filter," *Electron. Lett.,* vol. 33, no. 25, 1997, pp. 2147–2148.

[123] M. K. Smit and C. van Dam, "PHASAR-Based WDM-Devices: Principles, Design and Application," *IEEE J. Sel. Topics Quant. Electron.,* vol. 2, no. 2, 1996, pp. 236–250.

[124] Y. K. Chen and C. C. Lee, "Fiber Bragg Grating-Based Large Nonblocking Multiwavelength Cross-Connects," *J. Lightwave Technol.,* vol. 16, no. 10, 1998, pp. 1746–1756.

[125] S. Suzuki et al., "A Photonic Wavelength-Division Switching System Using Tunable Laser Diode Filters," *IEEE ICC'89 Conference Records,* Boston, 1989, paper 23.1.

[126] A. Dragone, "Efficient $N \times N$ Star Couplers Using Fourier Optics," *J. Lightwave Technol.,* vol. 7, 1989, pp. 479–489.

[127] K. Y. Eng, M. A. Santoro, T. L. Koch, J. Stone, and W. W. Snell, "Star-Coupler-Based Optical Cross-Connect Switch Experiments with Tunable Receivers," *IEEE JSAC,* vol. 8, no. 6, 1990, pp. 1026–1031.

[128] K. Kato et al., "Packaging of Large-Scale Integrated Optic $N \times N$ Star Couplers," *IEEE Photon. Technol. Lett.,* vol. 4, no. 33, 1993, pp. 348–351.

[129] N. A. Jackman, S. H. Patel, B. P. Mikkelsen, and S. K. Korotky, "Optical Cross Connect for Optical Networking," *Bell Labs Tech. J.,* vol. 4, no. 1, 1999, pp. 262–281.

[130] H. Takahashi et al., "Arrayed-Waveguide Grating for Wavelength Division Multiplexing/Demultiplexing with Nanometer Resolution," *Electron. Lett.,* vol. 26, 1990, pp. 87–88.

[131] H. Rokugawa et al., "Wavelength Conversion Laser Diodes Application to Wavelength-Division Photonic Cross-Connect Node with Multistage Configuration," *IEICE Trans. Commun.,* vol. E-75-B, no. 4, 1992, pp. 267–273.

[132] T. G. Robertazzi, Ed., *Performance Evaluation of High Speed Switching Fabrics and Networks,* IEEE Press, New York, 1993.

[133] A. Budman et al., "Multi-Gigabit Optical Packet Switch for Self-Routing Networks with Subcarrier Addressing," *Proc. OFC'92, Conference,* San Jose, CA, Feb. 1992, paper Tu04.

[134] A. Hunter and D. Smith, "New Architecture for Optical TDM Switching," *J. Lightwave Technol.,* vol. 11, no. 3, 1993, pp. 495–511.

[135] B. Nussbaum, "Communication Network Needs and Technologies—A Place for Photonic Switching," *IEEE JSAC,* vol. 6, no. 7, 1988, pp. 1036–1043.

[136] S. A. Cassidy and P. Yennadhiou, "Optimum Switching Architectures Using D-Fiber Optical Space Switches," *IEEE JSAC,* vol. 6, no. 7, 1988, pp. 1044–1051.

[137] C. J. Smith, "Nonblocking Photonic Switch Networks," *IEEE JSAC,* vol. 6, no. 7, 1988, pp. 1052–1062.

[138] J. D. Evankow, Jr. and R. A. Thompson, "Photonic Switching Modules Designed with Laser Diode Amplifiers," *IEEE JSAC,* vol. 6, no. 7. 1988, pp. 1087–1095.

[139] K. Y. Eng, "A Photonic Knockout Switch for High-Speed Packet Networks," *IEEE JSAC,* vol. 6, no. 7, 1988, pp. 1107–1116.

[140] R. C. Alferness, "Waveguide Electrooptic Switch Arrays," *IEEE JSAC,* vol. 6, no. 7, 1988, pp. 1117–1130.

[141] T. Ikegami and H. Kawaguchi, "Semiconductor Devices in Photonic Switching," *IEEE JSAC,* vol. 6, no. 7, 1988, pp. 1131–1140.

[142] R. I. Macdonald, "Terminology for Photonic Matrix Switches," *IEEE JSAC,* vol. 6, no. 7, 1988, pp. 1141–1151.

[143] J. V. Wright, S. R. Mallinson, and C. A. Millar, "A Fiber-Based Crosspoint Switch Using High-Refractive Index Interlay Materials," *IEEE JSAC,* vol. 6, no. 7, 1988, pp. 1160–1168.

[144] J. Skinner and C. H. R. Lane, "A Low-Crosstalk Microoptic Liquid Crystal Switch," *IEEE JSAC,* vol. 6, no. 7, 1988, pp. 1178–1185.

[145] T. Morioka and M. Saruwatari, "Ultrafast All-Optical Switching Utilizing the Optical Kerr Effect in Polarization-Maintaining Single-Mode Fibers," *IEEE JSAC,* vol. 6, no. 7, 1988, pp. 1186–1198.

[146] H. S. Hinton, "Architectural Considerations for Photonic Switching Networks," *IEEE JSAC,* vol. 6, no. 7, 1988, pp. 1209–1226.

[147] H. Inoue, H. Nakamura, K. Morosawa, Y. Sasaki, T. Katsuyama, and N. Chinone, "An 8 mm Length Nonblocking 4 × 4 Optical Switch Array," *IEEE JSAC,* vol. 6, no. 7, 1988, pp. 1262–1266.

[148] D. J. Bishop and V. A. Aksyuk, "Optical MEMS Answer High-Speed Networking Requirements," *Electron. Design,* Apr. 5, 1999, pp. 85–92.

[149] A. Brauer and P. Dannberg, "Polymers for Passive and Switching Waveguide Components for Optical Communication," in *Polymers in Optics: Physics, Chemistry, and Applications,* R. A. Lessard and W. F. Frank, Eds., SPIE, Bellingham, WA, 1996, pp. 334–348

[150] C. R. Doerr, "Proposed WDM Cross Connect Using a Planar Arrangement of Waveguide Grating Routers and Phase Shifters," *IEEE Photon. Technol. Lett.,* vol. 10, 1998, pp. 528–530.

[151] H. Rokugawa et al., "Wavelength Conversion Laser Diodes Application to Wavelength-Division Photonic Cross-Connect Node with Multistage Configuration," *IEICE Trans. Commun.,* vol. E-75-B, no. 4, 1992, pp. 267–273.

[152] T. G. Robertazzi, Ed., *Performance Evaluation of High Speed Switching Fabrics and Networks,* IEEE Press, New York, 1993.

[153] Y. K. Chen and C. C. Lee, "Fiber Bragg Grating-Based Large Nonblocking Multiwavelength Cross-Connects," *J. Lightwave Technol.,* vol. 16, no. 10, 1998, pp. 1746–1756.

[154] J. E. Ford, V. A. Aksyuk, D. J. Bishop, and J. A. Walker, "Wavelength Add/Drop Switching Using Tilting Micromirrors," *J. Lightwave Technol.,* vol. 17, no. 5, 1999, pp. 904–911.

[155] C. R. Giles and M. Spector, "The Wavelength Add/Drop Multiplexer for Lightwave Communication Networks," *Bell Labs Tech. J.,* vol. 4, no. 1, 1999, pp. 207–229.

[156] S. Suzuki et al., "A Photonic Wavelength-Division Switching System Using Tunable Laser Diode Filters," *IEEE ICC'89 Conference Records,* Boston, 1989, paper 23.1.

[157] Y. Pan, C. Qiao, and Y. Yang, "Optical Multistage Interconnection Networks: New Challenges and Approaches," *IEEE Commun. Mag.,* vol. 37, no 2, 1999, pp. 50–56.

[158] H. Hinton, *An Introduction to Photonic Switching Fabrics,* Plenum, New York, 1993.

[159] A. Tocci and H. J. Caufield, *Optical Interconnection-Foundations and Applications,* Artech House, Boston, 1994.

STANDARDS .

[1] ANSI/IEEE 812-1984, "Definition of Terms Relating to Fiber Optics," 1984.

[2] ITU-T Recommendation G.650, "Definition and Test Methods for the Relevant Parameters of Single-Mode Fibres," 1996.

[3] ITU-T Recommendation G.652, version 4, "Characteristics of a Single-Mode Optical Fiber Cable," Apr. 1997.

[4] ITU-T Recommendation G.653, version 4, "Characteristics of a Dispersion-Shifted Single-Mode Optical Fiber Cable," Apr. 1997.

[5] ITU-T Recommendation G.655, version 10, "Characteristics of a Non-Zero Dispersion-Shifted Single-Mode Optical Fiber Cable," Oct. 1996.

[6] ITU-T Recommendation G.661, "Definition and Test Methods for the Relevant Generic Parameters of Optical Fiber Amplifiers," Nov. 1996.

[7] ITU-T Recommendation G.662, "Generic Characteristics of Optical Fiber Amplifier Devices and Sub-Systems," July 1995.

[8] ITU-T Recommendation G.663, "Application Related Aspects of Optical Fiber Amplifier Devices and Sub-Systems," July 1995.

[9] ITU-T Recommendation G.671, "Transmission Characteristics of Passive Optical Components," Nov. 1996.

[10] ITU-T Recommendation G.702, "Digital Hierarchy Bit Rates," 1988.

[11] ITU-T Recommendation G.741, "General Considerations on Second Order Multiplex Equipments," 1988.

[12] ITU-T Recommendation G.911, "Parameters and Calculation Methodologies for Reliability and Availability of Fibre Optic Systems," 1997.

[13] Go to http://www.itu.int/ITU-T/index.html for a list of ITU standards.

[14] Telcordia GR-63-CORE, "Network Equipment Building System (NEBS)—Generic Equipment Requirements," Oct. 1995.

[15] Telcordia GR-1221-CORE, "Generic Reliability Assurance Requirements for Fiber Optic Branching Components," Jan. 1999.

[16] Telcordia GR-1312-CORE, "Generic Requirements for OFAs and Proprietary DWDM Systems," Apr. 1999.

[17] Telcordia TR-NWT-000468, "Reliability Assurance Practices for Optoelectronic Devices in Central Office Applications," Dec. 1998.

[18] Telcordia TR-NWT-917, "Regenerator," Oct. 1990.

CHAPTER 3

PARAMETERS AFFECTING THE OPTICAL DWDM SIGNAL

3.1 INTRODUCTION

Transporting Synchronous Optical Network (SONET) OC-768 at 40 Gbps [or the Synchronous Digital Hierarchy (SDH) equivalent] signals over a single-mode fiber in excess of 100 km is a technology that is becoming readily available. Advancements in *dense wavelength-division multiplexing* (DWDM) technology have made it possible to transmit more than 200 wavelengths in the same fiber, and the projections are that we will soon see 1000 wavelengths. However, although DWDM technology will enable the optical network of the near future to transport astonishing aggregate bandwidths, the network must demonstrate comparable reliability, scalability and availability.

The availability of a network depends by and large on the availability of the nodes in the network, including the fiber links and the optical components (e.g., filters and amplifiers) between transmitters (sources) and receivers (photodetectors). In addition, it depends on the system's ability to quickly detect degradations and/or faults that impact the quality of signal and the remedial action it takes. Thus, degradations and/or faults, which affect the deliverability and the quality of a client's signal must be monitored. Fault monitoring, detection, correlation, and localization in DWDM systems and networks can be complex, because the optical signal is not easy to monitor with nonintrusive methods and the degradable parameters of optical components are many.

The objective of this chapter is to identify the parameters of components that when they degrade and/or fail affect the optical signal. In subsequent chapters we examine the degradation and failure mechanisms of optical components, their correlations, and the action initiated.

3.2 COMPONENT PARAMETERS

The functional and transmission characteristics of optical components are affected by several parameters, some common to all and some specific to a particular class

51

of components. In addition, degradation and failure of an integrated electronic component that affects the functional operation of an active optical sub-component, such as a tunable filter, or a coupler, or a MEMS fabric, is also considered a failure of the optical component.

It is desirable that most optical component degradations and faults are directly detected in the optical regime. However, in many cases this may not be possible or cost-effective, and faulty conditions or their symptoms are detected by converting optical information into electrical first; two examples are cross-talk and bit error rate.

An optical cross-connect (OXC), or an optical add-drop multiplexer (OADM), passive or active, are considered components that provide the corresponding function and not complex subsystems. Because some classes of optical components are based on the same principles of physics, such as OFAs (EDFA and PDFA), we examine them on the aggregate.

Standards, such as ITU-T G.650 (which lists more related standards) and IEC-1300-3-4 to IEC-1300-3-19 provide a list of parameters and recommend measuring methodologies. In the following, we enhance the list and identify with an asterisk those parameters that are not mentioned and are worth reexamining.

3.2.1 Parameters Common to All Optical Components

- Insertion loss (IL)
- Optical reflectance
- Operating wavelength range
- Polarization-dependent loss
- Polarization-dependant wavelength (variable)*
- Polarization-dependent reflectance
- Isotropy/anisotropy of refracting material*
- Isotropy/anisotropy of defracting material*
- Birefringence of optical material*
- Effect of temperature, pressure, and humidity on component*
- Effect of vibration (G max) on component*
- Effect of electromagnetic field on component*
- Typical & min-max operating conditions*
- Mechanical (flex, twist, side and longitudinal pull, etc.)*

---

*These parameters are not included in the list of G.650.

3.2.2 Parameters Specific to Branching Optical Components

- Parameters related to directivity[†] of branching light
- Parameters related to uniformity[‡] of branching light
- Branching light variation over time*

3.2.3 Parameters Specific to Mux/Demux Optical Components

- Wavelength-dependent attenuation
- Spatial distribution of power per wavelength*
- Sensitivity of wavelength directivity*
- Far-end cross-talk
- Near-end cross-talk

3.2.4 Parameters Specific to Optical Attenuators

- Insertion loss tolerance
- Attenuation range (variable attenuation)
- Incremental attenuation (variable attenuation)
- Spectral attenuation distribution per channel*
- Polarization shift*

3.2.5 Parameters Specific to Optical Filters

- Backward loss
- Polarization mode dispersion
- Modulation depth (modulated light)
- Output light intensity (OCh optical power)*
- Finesse [Fabry-Perot (FP) filter]*
- Spectral width*
- Line width*
- Cutoff λ*

---

*These parameters are not included in the list of G.650.

[†]Directivity is the power transferred from input to output.

[‡]Uniformity is the maximum variation of IL between one input and any two outputs, or between any two inputs and one output.

- Extinction ratio*
- Line spacing*

3.2.6 Parameters Specific to Optical Switches

- Min-max switching time per element in the matrix*
- Min-max loss distribution per element in the matrix*
- Repeatability
- Uniformity
- Cross-talk
- Directivity
- Extinction ratio*
- Transfer matrix
- Doppler shift (in mechanical switches)*

3.2.7 Parameters Specific to Passive Dispersion Compensation†

- Dispersion over operating λ range
- Polarization mode dispersion
- Polarization dependent loss*

3.2.8 Parameters Specific to Fibers*

The following list is per fiber type [e.g., single-mode fiber (SMF), dispersion compensation fiber (DCF), Pigtail]

- Forward attenuation/km
- Backward attenuation/km (if asymmetric)
- Polarization mode dispersion
- Polarization-dependent loss (PDL)
- Dispersion (chromatic and material)
- Zero-dispersion wavelength
- Dispersion flatness over spectrum range
- Birefringence
- Cutoff λ

---

*These parameters are not included in the list of G.650.
†Specified per fiber type and per component type.

3.2.9 Parameters Specific to Light Sources*

- OCh output power
- OCh wavelength λ_0
- Line spacing
- Cutoff λ (tunable sources)
- Tunability speed (tunable sources)
- Spectral width (tunable sources)
- Line width (light sources)
- Modulation depth (modulated sources)
- Bit rate (max-min) (modulated sources)
- Source noise
- Dependency on bias

3.2.10 Parameters Specific to Receivers*

- Minimum threshold optical power, minimum sensitivity
- Responsiveness per wavelength, λ_0
- Wavelength discrimination
- Receiver bit rate (max-min)
- Min-max threshold level (one-zero)
- Dependency on ones density
- Dependence on polarization
- Demodulation
- Receiver noise
- Dependency on bias
- Dependency on temperature

REFERENCES

[1] S. V. Kartalopoulos, *Introduction to DWDM: Data in a Rainbow,* IEEE Press, New York, 2000.

[2] S. V. Kartalopoulos, *Understanding SONET/SDH and ATM: Communications Networks for the next Millennium,* IEEE Press, New York, 1999.

[3] R. Ramaswami and K. N. Sivarajan, *Optical Networks,* Morgan Kaufmann, San Francisco, CA, 1998.

*These parameters are not included in the list of G.650.

[4] B. Mukherjee, *Optical Communication Networks,* McGraw-Hill, New York, 1997.

[5] I. P. Kaminow, Ed., and T. L. Koch, Ed., *Optical Fiber Communications IIIA* and *Optical Fiber Communications IIIB,* Academic, New York, 1997.

[6] J. C. Palais, *Fiber Optic Communications,* 3rd ed., Prentice-Hall, Englewood Cliffs, NJ, 1992.

[7] R. G. Hunsperger, *Integrated Optics: Theory and Technology,* Springer-Verlag, New York, 1984.

[8] S. Sudo, Ed., *Optical Fiber Amplifiers: Materials, Devices, and Applications,* Artech House, Boston, 1997.

[9] J. Hecht, *The Laser Guidebook,* 2nd ed., Tab Books, Blue Ridge Summit, PA, 1992.

[10] T. Wildi, *Units and Conversion Charts,* 2nd ed., IEEE Press, New York, 1995.

[11] G. Hernandez, *Fabry-Perot Interferometers,* Cambridge University Press, Cambridge, 1986.

[12] P. S. Henry, "Lightwave Primer," *IEEE J. Quant. Electron.,* vol. QE-21, 1985, pp. 1862–1879.

[13] L. Kazovsky, S. Benedetto, and A. Willner, *Optical Fiber Communication Systems,* Artech House, Boston, 1996.

[14] J. C. Palais, *Fiber Optic Communications,* 3rd ed., Prentice-Hall, Englewood Cliffs, NJ, 1992.

[15] M. Francon, *Optique: formation et traitment des images,* Macon & Cie, Paris, 1972.

[16] T. G. Robertazzi, Ed., *Performance Evaluation of High Speed Switching Fabrics and Networks,* IEEE Press, New York, 1993.

STANDARDS

[1] ANSI/IEEE 812-1984, "Definition of Terms Relating to Fiber Optics, 1984."

[2] ITU-T Recommendation G.650, "Definition and Test Methods for the Relevant Parameters of Single-Mode Fibres," 1996.

[3] ITU-T Recommendation G.652, version 4, "Characteristics of a Single-Mode Optical Fiber Cable," Apr. 1997.

[4] ITU-T Recommendation G.653, version 4, "Characteristics of a Dispersion-Shifted Single-Mode Optical Fiber Cable," Apr. 1997.

[5] ITU-T Recommendation G.655, version 10, "Characteristics of a Non-Zero Dispersion-Shifted Single-Mode Optical Fiber Cable," Oct. 1996.

[6] ITU-T Recommendation G.661, "Definition and Test Methods for the Relevant Generic Parameters of Optical Fiber Amplifiers," Nov. 1996.

[7] ITU-T Recommendation G.662, "Generic Characteristics of Optical Fiber Amplifier Devices and Sub-Systems," July 1995.

[8] ITU-T Recommendation G.663, "Application Related Aspects of Optical Fiber Amplifier Devices and Sub-Systems," July 1995.

[9] ITU-T Recommendation G.671, "Transmission Characteristics of Passive Optical Components," Nov. 1996.

[10] ITU-T Recommendation G.821, "Error Performance of an International Digital Con-

nection Operating at a Bit Rate Below the Primary Rate and Forming Part of an Integrated Services Digital Network," Aug. 1996.

[11] ITU-T Recommendation G.826, "Error Performance Parameters and Objectives for International, Constant Bit Rate Digital Paths at or Above the Primary Rate," Feb. 1999.

[12] ITU-T Recommendation G.828, "Error Performance Parameters and Objectives for International, Constant Bit Rate Synchronous Digital Paths," Feb. 2000.

[13] Go to http://www.itu.int/ITU-T/index.html for a list of ITU standards.

[14] Telcordia GR-1221-CORE, "Generic Reliability Assurance Requirements for Fiber Optic Branching Components," January 1999.

[15] Telcordia TR-NWT-233, "Digital Cross Connect System," Nov. 1992.

[16] Telcordia TR-NWT-000357, "Component Reliability Assurance—Generic Requirements for Telecommunications Equipment," October 1993.

[17] Telcordia TR-NWT-000468, "Reliability Assurance Practices for Optoelectronic Devices in Central Office Applications," December 1998.

[18] Telcordia TR-NWT-917, "Regenerator," Oct. 1990.

CHAPTER 4

FAULTS AFFECTING THE OPTICAL DWDM SIGNAL

4.1 INTRODUCTION

In general, the quality of (a digital) signal is a term related to the amount of altered bits in the signal, that is, 0s that are detected as 1s, and 1s as 0s. This happens either because added power (noise signal) changes the bits or because interactions between light and matter or between light-matter and light affect the integrity of the bits (signal distortion). Thus, in a DWDM system there is a variety of noise sources, such as, for example, laser noise, reflections, ASE, and receiver noise, as well as a variety of distortion sources, such as dispersion, PMD, FWM, and so on. Both types of sources (noise and distortion) add to the amount of errored bits, and the end result is an increase in the bit error rate (BER), cross-talk, or intersymbol interference (ISI). Unfortunately, when excessive BER is detected, it is not quite obvious which mechanism (noise or distortion) influenced the signal integrity and increased BER.

The signal integrity in DWDM systems becomes increasingly complex as DWDM evolves, having more optical channels, higher bit rates, and increasing fiber spans. Unfortunately, the signal quality in the optical domain is very difficult to monitor, and one resorts to monitoring the quality of the signal after it has been converted to an electrical signal. Once this is done, standard methodology and techniques are used to measure the quality of the signal, such as eye diagrams (including threshold levels, triggering points, and amplitude levels) and BER measurements. However, one has to keep in mind that the quality of the electrical signal is not an exact representation of the quality of the optical signal. The former consists of degradations due to photonic interactions and optics that are superimposed with degradations due to optoelectronic conversion (quantum efficiency, diode noise, and temperature) and due to electronic components [capacitors, resistors, temperature, board-layout cross-talk (ground loops), connector cross-talk, sampling clock stability, and electromagnetic interference]. Many of these degradations add to the noise content of the signal, rise- and fall-time distortions, spikes, signal ripple, ground floor noise, temporal shifts, and waveform skew.

The content of errored bits in a signal is a key parameter that must be continuously monitored. We cannot lose sight of the fact that the responsibility of communications systems and networks is to transport in a timely manner to the receiving terminal (the sink end user) the same bits that the transmitting end terminal (the source end user) has sent. To safeguard this, standards define performance parameters pertaining to the frequency of bit errors, such as error seconds (ESs), severe error seconds (SESs), and severely errored period intensity (SEPI), as well as how to measure and report these performance parameters (a task beyond the scope of this book).

In the previous chapter we identified and classified the various parameters that when degrade and/or fail affect the quality of the optical signal. The objective of this chapter is to examine the degradation and failure mechanisms of optical components, which affect the optical signal quality, and their detectability. It examines the observable optical parameters and the predictors that infer (with a high degree of probability/possibility) degradation or failure and the remedial actions to be taken. It adds to the fault management design process in systems and in networks.

Specifically:

A. We identify the observable parameters or predictors based on which component degradation or failure is determined.

B. We identify types of faults of optical components and hint on the action to be triggered. For example, a component may fail (e.g., no laser optical power is detected), it is detected, and a unit replacement action (or switch to protection) may be invoked. As another example, a component may be degraded (e.g., laser optical power drops or center wavelength drifts) to a level that may result in increased BER (bit error rate) and/or ISI (intersymbol interference). In this case, a unit replacement action (or switch to protection) may proactively be invoked.

C. We correlate faults to infer conditions that may not be directly observable. Certain degradation and failures are directly and conclusively detected (e.g., laser output power loss), whereas certain others are indirectly detected by fault correlation (e.g., is BER increased due to FWM contribution or due to pulse spreading and increased ASE or to some other photonic error source?).

Correlation and inference may invoke actions to locate a hidden fault and to isolate it within a node. As an example, the malfunction of one or more of the mirrors in MEMS may result either in output power loss of a corresponding channel and/or in excess BER and cross-talk of another channel. Similarly, center wavelength drifts may cause BER and cross-talk in one or more channels or received power degradation if a selective filter or an optical add-drop multiplexer is involved.

4.2 COMPONENTS

In this section we examine the fault detectability of the following optical components:

- Filters (Fabry-Perot, Bragg, chirped Bragg, acousto-optical)
- Amplifiers: SOA, OFA (EDFA)
- Optical Mux/Demux
- Optical switches: $LiNbO_3$, MEMS, liquid crystal (LC)
- OADM: $LiNbO_3$, MEMS-based
- Transmitters: laser-based
- Receivers: PIN, APD
- Fiber (multiwavelength fiber as a component)

The information provided about these components is formatted, as applicable, as follows:

- The *functional entity* in which the component may reside
- *Measurable* and *degradable* parameters of the component
- *Potential faults* and how they *impact* system performance
- *Fault observability* (symptoms) and *fault detectability*
- System *action*
- Related *comments*

4.3 FILTERS: FABRY-PEROT (PASSIVE, FIXED)

Function Entity. Receiver unit, optical transponder unit, optical demultiplexer, optical add-drop multiplexer, and λ isolation or λ monitoring.

Measurable Parameters	Degradable Parameters
Number of OChs	—
λ_0 per OCh	λ_0 per OCh due to temperature, stress, or field variations
Line width	Line width due to temperature, stress, or field variations

Measurable Parameters	Degradable Parameters
Channel separation	Line spacing due to temperature, stress, or field variations
Spectral width (cutoff wavelengths)	Due to temperature, stress, or field variations
Power amplitude per OCh (at λ_0) gain	Power amplitude (at λ_0) due to temperature, stress, or field variations
Polarization shift	Polarization shift due to temperature, stress, or field variations; extinction ratio
Polarization-dependent loss (PDL)	Optical channel power
Filter finesse or sharpness	Finesse due to temperature or field variations
Component temperature (°C)	Alters most filter parameters

Potential Faults	Impact
Temperature, stress, or field variations	Affect filter constants (d, n, and R) and filter specifications, λ_0 per OCh, insertion loss per OCh, potential BER per OCh increase, potential cross-talk and extinction ratio

Fault Observability (Symptoms)

- BER due to excessive spread of line width and/or optical power degradation
- BER due to polarization-dependent losses
- Cross-talk due to line-width spread
- Signal degradation at receiver BER (when optical power lowers)
- Signal loss (if optical power falls below receiver's quantum limit)

Fault Detectability (from a System Viewpoint)

- λ_0/OCh shift [detected via tapped Demux, error detection coding (EDC), and/or test signals] [Note that EDC requires optical-to-electrical (O-E) conversion.]
- Optical power level of all channels drops (detected via EDC and/or test signals)
- Optical power level of channel drops unevenly (some more than others due to filter spectral response)

- BER per channel increase (detected via in-band EDC)
- Cross-talk per two adjacent channels (detected via EDC and/or test signals)

Comments

- Fabry-Perot (FP) filter has very good finesse.
- Filter finesse depends on reflectivity.
- It has compact design (single thin plate).
- Stability of material is very good.
- FP may be integrated with other optical components.

4.4   FILTERS: FIBER BRAGG GRATING (PASSIVE, FIXED)

Function Entity.   Receivers, optical transponder unit, optical Demux, optical add-drop Mux, λ isolation or λ monitoring.

Measurable Parameters	Degradable Parameters
Number of OChs in and out	Number of OChs out (at either port)
λ_0 per OCh out	λ_0 per OCh due to temperature, stress, or field variations
Line width per OCh out	Line width due to temperature, stress, or field variations
Line spacing of OCh out	Line spacing due to temperature or field variations
Power amplitude per OCh (at λ_0)	Power amplitude (at λ_0) due to temperature, stress, or field variations
Insertion loss per OCh (dB at λ_0)	Insertion loss per output (per OCh)
Polarization shift per OCh	Polarization shift due to temperature, stress, or field variations; extinction ratio
Polarization-dependent loss (PDL)	Optical channel power
Filter finesse or sharpness	Finesse due to temperature, stress, or field variations
Component temperature (°C)	Alters grating parameters and thus its performance

Potential Faults	Impact
Temperature, stress, or field variations	Affect filter constants (d, n) and filter specs, λ_0 per OCh, insertion loss per OCh, BER per OCh, dispersion characteristics per OCh and extinction ratio

Fault Observability (Symptoms)

- BER due to excessive spread of line width and/or optical power degradation
- Cross-talk due to excessive line-width spread
- Signal degradation at receiver BER (when optical power lowers)
- Signal loss (when optical power falls below receiver's quantum limit)

Fault Detectability (from a System Viewpoint)

- λ_0/OCh shifts (detected via EDC and/or test signals)
- Optical power level of all channel drops (detected via EDC and/or test signals)
- Optical power level of channels drops unevenly (some more than others due to filter spectral response)
- BER per channel increases (detected via in-band EDC)
- Cross-talk per two adjacent channels (detect via EDC and/or test signals)

Comment	Benefits
Fiber Bragg filters are compact.	Connected in-line with the transmission fiber or other component Require fiber connector or fusion with fiber May be integrated with other optical components

4.5 FILTERS: CHIRPED FBG (PASSIVE, FIXED)

Function Entity. Receivers, optical transponder unit, optical Demux, dispersion component, optical add-drop Mux, λ isolation or λ monitoring.

Measurable Parameters	Degradable Parameters
Number of OChs in and out	Number of OChs out (at either port)
λ_0 per OCh out	λ_0 per OCh due to temperature, stress, or field variations
Line width per OCh out	Line width due to temperature, stress, or field variations
Line spacing of OCh out	Line spacing due to temperature or field variations
Power amplitude per OCh (at λ_0)	Power amplitude (at λ_0) due to temperature, stress, or field variations
Insertion loss per OCh (dB at λ_0)	Insertion loss per OCh out
Polarization shift per OCh	Polarization shift due to temperature, stress, or field variations; extinction ratio
Polarization-dependent loss (PDL)	Optical channel power
Filter finesse or sharpness	Finesse due to temperature, stress, or field variations
Component temperature (°C)	Alters grating parameters and thus its performance

Potential Faults	Impact
Temperature, stress, or field variations	Variations of filter constants (d, n) affect filter specifications Affect λ_0 per OCh, insertion loss per OCh, BER per OCh, and dispersion characteristics per OCh, and extinction ratio

Fault Observability (Symptoms)

- BER due to excessive spread of line width and/or optical power degradation
- Cross-talk due to excessive line-width spread
- Signal degradation at receiver BER (when optical power lowers)
- Signal loss (when optical power falls below receiver's quantum limit)

Fault Detectability (from a System Viewpoint)

- λ_0/OCh shifts (detected via EDC and/or test signals)
- Optical power level of all channels drops (detected via EDC and/or test signals)

- Optical power level of channels drops unevenly (some more than others due to filter spectral response)
- BER per channel increases (detected via in-band EDC)
- Cross-talk per two adjacent channels (detected via EDC and/or test signals)

Comment	Benefits
Chirped Bragg filters are compact.	May be integrated with other optical components Filtered out OCh compensated for dispersion Connected in-line with the transmission fiber or other component Requires fiber connector or fusion with fiber

4.6   FILTERS: ACOUSTO-OPTIC TUNABLE Ti:LiNbO₃

Function Entity.   Receivers, optical transponder unit, optical Demux, optical add-drop Mux, λ broadcast, TE-TM converter, λ isolation or monitoring.

Measurable Parameters	Degradable Parameters
Tuning range	Range depends on filter (several nanometers or ~1 μm)
Wavelength resolution	Wavelength resolution (on the order of 0.01 nm)
Insertion loss	Output power
Filter bandwidth	Filter bandwidth
Cross-talk	Signal-to-noise ratio (S/N)
IF frequency shift	Wavelength stability
Component temperature	Filter characteristics
Polarization	Polarization varies with temperature or voltage variations; extinction ratio
Polarization-dependent loss (PDL)	PDL varies with frequency (f), temperature, or voltage variations
Component temperature	Alters surface acoustic wave (SAW) filter parameters and thus its performance

Potential Faults	Impact
Misalignment of polarization state	Polarization mismatch that results in coupling loss
Frequency shift due to Doppler effect	Wavelength registration mismatch*
RF shift	Alters Bragg constant and filter tuning
RF power change (mW)	Alters polarization state
Temperature increase	Alters active area characteristics, passband, polarization, λ registration, and access time

*Not applicable in all implementations.

Fault Observability (Symptoms)

- BER increase due to λ misregistration
- BER increase due to OCh power decrease affected by RF power variations
- BER increase and OCh power level decrease due to change in polarization state*
- Temperature changes alter all filter characteristics and specifications (BER, cross-talk, S/N)
- Increased insertion loss increases BER
- Increased cross-talk decreases S/N
- S/N decrease, BER increase, and cross-talk increase due to slow tunability

Fault Detectability (from a System Viewpoint)

- Increased IL (detected via EDC and/or test signals)
- Decreased S/N (detected via EDC and/or test signals)
- λ_0/OCh shifts due to component parametric changes of RF changes (detected via EDC and/or test signals)
- Output power level drop (detected via EDC and/or test signals)
- Increased BER (detected via in-band EDC)
- Increased cross-talk per two adjacent channels (detected via EDC and/or test signals)

*Not applicable in all implementations (two stage).

Comments	Benefits
Solid-state construction	Low cross-talk, < -20 dB
Broad tuning range	One to many wavelength selection
Narrow filter bandwidth, <1 nm	Possible wavelength broadcast
Fast tunability, ~10 μs	Easy wavelength registration and stabilization
Acceptable insertion loss, <5 dB	—

4.7   SOA: InGaAsP

Function Entity.   Optical amplifier, postamplifier (after optical transmitter), preamplifier (before optical receiver), amplification within compound component (e.g., Mux/Demux, OADM).

Measurable Parameters*	Degradable Parameters
Injection current	Applied voltage (pump)
Input power range	—
Output power range	Output power
Noise figure (ASE)	S/N
Center frequency (at output)	Center frequency; line width
Gain per OCh (at output)	Gain per OCh
Polarization	Extinction ratio
Component temperature	Alters SOA parameters and thus its λ_0 and output power

*See ITU-T Recommendation G.662 for amplifier classifications and device characteristics.

Potential Faults	Impact
Injection current change	Gain degradation, cross-talk, increased noise, possible loss of signal (LOS)
Coupling inefficiency	Loss of gain, increased BER, possible LOS
Temperature increase	Gain, output power, line width, polarization, cross-talk, noise; temperature shifts λ and degrades power level

Fault Observability (Symptoms)

- Signal degradation at receiver; increased BER; cross-talk due to gain degradation/lost
- Signal degradation at receiver; decreased S/N due to gain degradation/lost
- Signal degradation at receiver; due to polarization effects

Fault Detectability (from a System Viewpoint)

- Decreased S/N ratio (detected via EDC)
- Increased BER (detected via in-band EDC)
- Loss of signal (detected via power loss detector)
- λ_0 shifts due to component parametric changes (detected via EDC and/or test signals)
- Output power level drops (detected via EDC and/or test signals)
- Increased cross-talk (detected via EDC and/or test signals)

Comments	Benefits
They are compact.	They operate in the regions of 0.8, 1.3, and 1.5 μm and have high gain factor (~20 dB).
	They are integrable into arrays and with other components.
SOAs are polarization dependent.	They may require polarization-maintaining fiber or circular polarizers.
They may be used as λ converters.	—
They may be used as modulator/amplifiers.	In certain applications they eliminate the need for amplification.
They have an output saturation power in the range of 5–10 dBm.	They can be tunable and have large bandwidth.
They have high noise figure and high cross-talk level due to nonlinearities.	They require good coupling with fiber [use antireflecting (AR) coating].

4.8   OFA: FACTORS AFFECTING INTEGRITY AND QUALITY OF SIGNAL

Optical fiber amplifiers are fibers heavily doped with a rare-earth element [erbium (EDFA), praseodimium (PDFA), thulium and fluoride (ThDFA), and a mix of erbium and titanium fiber amplifiers]. They operate on principles underlined by nonlinear phenomena, ion excitation, and stimulated emission of light. Ions are excited by one (or two) high-power laser(s) and the pump, and they are stimulated by the passing photons of a weak signal, thus adding photons to the signal and amplifying it; the pumps(s) emit light at different wavelengths. However, excited OFAs may emit spontaneously light, known as amplifier spontaneous emission (ASE), that adds to the noise of the signal (and thus decreases the S/N ratio). In this case, rejection optical filters and isolators must be used to remove the wavelength of the pump(s).

In the following, we examine the factors that affect nonlinearities and polarization properties related to the transmission characteristics of OFAs (see ITU-T Recommendation G.663) and controlling mechanisms. We also examine the single- and double-pump OFAs (EDFA and PDFA). No discrimination among pre-, post-, or line-amplifiers is made here.

Optical Nonlinearities

- *Stimulated Raman scattering (SRS):* OChs (at ~1 W) may behave as a pump for longer wavelengths or ASE degrading S/N ratio of other OChs. Not a well-known controlling mechanism.

- *Stimulated Brillouin scattering (SBS):* Threshold <5–10 mW (external mode), <20–30 mW (direct mode). Controlled by lowering signal intensity or make source line width wider than Brillouin bandwidth (BW).

- *Four-wave mixing (FWM):* Created sidebands may deplete OCh signal power. Controlled by channel spacing selection (wide or uneven selection).

- *Modulation instability (MI):* May reduce S/N due to created sidebands (and thus decrease optical power level).

- *Self-phase modulation (SPM):* Optical intensity changes change phase of signal; this broadens the signal spectrum (pulse width). Operating in the anomalous dispersion region, chromatic dispersion and SPM compensate each other. This may result in spontaneous formation of solitons.

- *Cross-phase modulation (XPM):* Interacting adjacent OChs induce phase changes and thus pulse broadening. Controlled by selecting convenient channel spacing.

Polarization Properties

- *Polarization mode dispersion (PMD):* It changes randomly the polarization state of a pulse, causing pulse broadening. Controlled by polarization scramblers, polarization controllers, or fiber selection.

- *Polarization-dependent loss (PDL):* Due to dichroism of optical components. It affects S/N and *Q*-value at the receiver. It may be controlled with polarization modulation techniques.

- *Polarization hole burning (PHB):* The selective depopulation of excited states due to anisotropic saturation by a polarized saturating signal in EDFA causes noise buildup. Controlled with depolarized signals or polarization scramblers.

Other

- *Dispersion properties:* OFAs exhibit all fiber properties, including dispersion.

- *Noise accumulation:* ASE noise is amplified by subsequent OFAs and thus is cumulative; it may exceed signal level (S/N > 1) or surpass the 0/1 discrimination ability of the receiver.

- *Temperature variations:* Some temperature-sensitive components may require component temperature stabilization (e.g., lasers, receivers) to maintain operation within the specified parameters. Some others may operate within a range of temperature (e.g., 0–70°C) and only environmental conditioning may be required.

4.9   OFA: SINGLE PUMP

Function Entity.   Optical in-line amplifier.

Measurable Parameters	Degradable Parameters
Pump wavelength	Pump wavelength may drift
Pump power	Pump power level
Spectral width (at output)	Spectral width
Gain	Gain per OCh
Gain differential across range	Optical power per wavelength not flat
S/N	ASE adds to noise floor
Temperature	Alters fiber parameters and thus its gain and flatness response as well as pump efficiency and thus OFA gain and flatness response

Potential Faults	Impact
Pump wavelength drift	Gain decrease of certain λs, possible LOS of certain OChs
Pump inoperable	Loss of gain, increased BER, possible LOS of all OChs
Pump power decreases	Gain decrease, increased BER, possible LOS of certain OChs
Pump power increases	Nonlinear effects, increased BER and cross-talk
Gain of OChs degrades	Possible increased BER and LOS of OChs
Gain of certain OCh degrades more than others	Possible increased BER and LOS of degraded OChs
Coupler malfunctioning	Loss of gain, increased BER, possible LOS of all OChs increased
ASE	Increased S/N ratio, increased BER
Nonlinearities on certain λs	Increased BER and cross-talk
Temperature increase	Degrades coupler, isolator, and fiber parameters

Fault Observability (Symptoms)

- Signal degradation at receiver: increased cross-talk due to pump power degradation/lost and decreased S/N ratios due to increased ASE
- Signal loss due to gain lost and uncompensated power loss

Fault Detectability (from a System Viewpoint)

- Pump power loss (detected by pump-monitoring device, or via EDC of all OChs, LOS)
- Pump saturates OFA [detected by excessive BER, loss of (eye) signal but no loss of optical power]
- Increased BER (detected via EDC, some or all OChs)
- Loss of signal (typically of all OChs)

Comments	Benefits
OFAs have good gain factor.	EDFA performs best in the C-band (1528–1561 nm).
	Erbium-titanium EDFAs perform best in the C- and L-bands (1561–1620 nm).
	PDFA performs best in the 1350–1528-nm range.
	Thulium-doped fluoride fiber amplifier performs best in the range about 1470 nm.
Gain control is required.	Optical equilizer at the receiver may be required.
Attenuation control is required to not optically stress the fiber.	OChs may suffer degradation due to FWM. Cross-phase modulation (XPM) and SRS may be required.
Fault localization strategy is needed.	Channel equalization may be required.
OFAs with Pr and Er-Ti are more difficult to manufacture than EDFA.	—

4.10 OFA: DOUBLE PUMP

Function Entity. In-line direct optical amplification (replaces regenerators), postamplifiers, preamplifiers.

Measurable Parameters	Degradable Parameters
Per-pump wavelength	Wavelength of each pump may drift
Per-pump power	Power of each pump; pump power differential
Spectral width (at output)	Spectral width
Gain	Gain per OCh
Gain differential over spectral range	Optical power per wavelength not flat
S/N	ASE adds to noise floor
Temperature	Alters fiber parameters and thus its gain and flatness response as well as pump efficiency and thus OFA gain and flatness response

Potential Faults	Impact
Pump wavelength drift	Gain degradation of certain λs, possible LOS of certain OChs
Pump inoperable	Loss of gain, increased BER, possible LOS of all OChs
Pump power decreases	Gain degradation, increased BER, possible LOS of certain OChs
Pump power increases	Strong nonlinear effects, increased BER and cross-talk
Gain of OChs degrades	Possible increased BER and LOS of OChs
Gain of certain OChs degrades more than others	Possible increased BER and LOS of degraded OChs
Coupler malfunctioning	Loss of gain, increased BER, possible LOS of all OChs
Increased ASE	Increased S/N ratio, increased BER
Nonlinearities on certain λs	Increased BER and cross-talk
Temperature increase	Degrades coupler, isolator and fiber parameters, degrades pump

Fault Observability (Symptoms)

- Signal degradation at receiver; increased crosstalk due to pump power degradation/lost
- Signal degradation at receiver; decreased S/N due to increased ASE
- Signal loss due to gain lost and uncompensated power loss

Fault Detectability (from a System Viewpoint)

- Pump power loss (detected by pump-monitoring device, or via EDC of all OChs, LOS); pump saturates OFA [detected by excessive BER, loss of signal (eye) but not loss of optical power]
- Increased BER [detected via EDC, some or all OChs)]
- Loss of signal (mostly for all OChs)

Comments	Benefits
OFAs have a good gain factor.	EDFA performs best in the C-band (1528–1561 nm). Erbium-titanium EDFAs perform best in the C- and L-band (1561–1620 nm). PDFA performs best in the 1350–1528-nm range. Thulium-doped fluoride fiber amplifier performs best in the range about 1470 nm.
Gain control is required.	Optical equilizer at the receiver may be required.
Attenuation control is required not to optically stress the fiber.	OChs may suffer degradation due to FWM. Cross-phase modulation (XPM) and SRS may be required.
Fault localization strategy is needed.	Channel equalization may be required.
It requires two pumps; EDFAs require 980 nm and 1480 nm at about <1 W.	Provides higher gain than a single pump.
It is more expensive than a single pump.	—
OFAs with Pr and Er-Ti are more difficult to manufacture than EDFA.	They perform above or beyond the range of EDFA.

4.11 MUX/DEMUX

Function Entity.   Wavelength Mux/Demux, optical line cards, optical cross-connects, optical add-drop multiplexers.

Measurable Parameters	Degradable Parameters
Wavelength resolution	λ resolution (separation between adjacent channel)
Number of optical channels	—
OCh width (line width)	Line-width spread
Polarization	Polarization mode change (rotation); extinction ratio
Polarization-dependent loss (PDL)	Power loss
Insertion loss	Insertion loss (per mirror)
Component temperature	Alters component parameters and thus its λ angular dispersion

Potential Faults	Impact
Wavelength discrimination	Separation between adjacent channel becomes fuzzy Eye diagram closes due to cross-talk and BER
Line-width spread	Power level per channel decreases; potential BER and cross-talk
Faulty coupler	LOS or signal degrade for all or some OChs
Polarization rotation	Affects signal power level; increases insertion loss
Temperature increase (depending on Mux/Demux technology)	Affects device parameters; possible phase shift, insertion loss per OCh

Fault Observability (Symptoms)

- Output signal level decrease at Demux output (per OCh)
- Output signal level decrease at Mux output (for all OChs)

Fault Detectability (from a System Viewpoint)

- Increased BER, one or few OChs (detected via EDC)
- Increased BER, all OChs (detected via EDC)
- Increased cross-talk (detected via EDC)
- Loss of signal, one or more OChs (via LOS detector)

Comments

- Mux/Demux is considered without optical amplifiers.
- If OAs are incorporated, then OA fault mechanisms should also be included.

4.12 OXC: MEMS

Function Entity.   Optical cross-connect, massive optical fabrics, core fabric.

Measurable Parameters	Degradable Parameters
OCh center wavelength	Negligible due to mirrors
OCh width (line width)	Negligible due to mirrors
Optical output power (OCh)	Power coupled to output (per OCh)
Polarization	Negligible due to mirrors
Switching speed (per mirror)	Switching speed
Insertion loss	Insertion loss (per mirror)
Component temperature	Alters component parameters and angular deflection

Potential Faults	Impact
Faulty mirror (stuck at one position)	Loss of OCh switching capability; possible BER and cross-talk increase in other OChs
Mirror does not rest at correct position	Degradation or possible loss of (OCh) power; increased insertion loss; possible BER and cross-talk increase in other OChs
Mirror oscillations (due to mirror or electrical noise)	Potential dispersion or jitter (due to Doppler?); possible BER and cross-talk increase in other OChs
Temperature increase	Affects all MEMS parameters; possible phase shift; insertion loss per OCh; potential channel interference

Fault Observability (Symptoms)

- OCh loss, one, few, or all
- OCh output power degradation, one, few, or all
- OCh switching capability loss, one, few, or all
- Mirror does not rest at correct position

Fault Detectability (from a System Viewpoint)

- Loss of OCh output power (detected via LOS detector)
- Increased insertion loss, one, few, or all OChs*
- Increased BER and cross-talk,* one, few, or all

Comments

- Not easy to test each mirror in-system; needs testing strategy
- Not easy to fault-manage large $N \times N$ MEMS ($N = 1000$?) on an OCh basis
- Protection MEMS possible but requires splitters

---

*An all-optical detection scheme is preferred. Currently, it is detected by EDC, which requires optical-to-electrical (O-E) conversion.

4.13   OXC: LiNbO₃

Function Entity.   Optical cross-connect, small OXCs, medium-size fast switching optical fabrics, wavelength distribution, small OADM.

Measurable Parameters	Degradable Parameters
OCh center wavelength	Not applicable
OCh width (line width)	Not applicable
Optical output power	Output power (per OCh)
Polarization	PMD per OCh
Channel switching speed (μs)	Negligible change; determined by manufacturer over the lifetime of component
Insertion loss (per OCh)	Insertion loss (per OCh)
Component temperature	Alters component parameters and thus cross-connected power and polarization state

Potential Faults	Impact
Faulty coupler	Loss of switching capability for several OChs; possible BER and cross-talk increase in other OCh
Temperature increase	Affects device parameters; possible phase shift, insertion loss per OCh

Fault Observability (Symptoms)

- OCh loss (one or more)
- OCh output power degradation
- OCh switching capability loss
- Increased cross-talk
- Increased PMD/PDL

Fault Detectability (from a System Viewpoint)

- Loss of OCh output power (detected via LOS)
- Increased insertion loss (detected via EDC)
- Increased BER and cross-talk (detected via EDC)

Comments

- Not easy to implement large $N \times N$ switches ($N = 64$?)
- Needs testing strategy
- Not easy to fault-manage large $N \times N$ switchers on an OCh basis
- Protection switch possible but requires splitters
- Requires cross-talk control
- Requires PMD/PDL control
- Requires equalization

4.14 OXC LIQUID CRYSTAL

Function Entity.   Optical cross-connect, small OXCs, small optical fabrics, wavelength distribution, small OADM, CWDM metro/access.

Measurable Parameters	Degradable Parameters
OCh center wavelength	Not applicable
OCh width (line width)	Not applicable
Number of cross-connects ($N \times N$)	Cross-connecting pixel
Optical output power (OCh)	Output power (per OCh)
Polarization	PMD per OCh
Switching speed (ms)	Switching speed; determined by manufacturer over lifetime of component
Insertion loss (per OCh)	Insertion loss (per OCh)
Uniformity of in-out delay	—
Component (LC matrix) temperature and pressure	Alters all component parameters

Potential Faults	Impact
Faulty coupler	Loss of switching capability for several OChs; possible BER and cross-talk increase in other OChs
Cross-connect failure	Loose channel connectivity; blocking
Temperature deviation from $T_{operational}$	Affects all device parameters (reflectivity, IL, polarization, switching speed)
Pressure deviation from $P_{operational}$	Affects all device parameters (reflectivity, IL, polarization, switching speed)

Fault Observability (Symptoms)

- OCh power loss (one or more)
- OCh output power degradation
- OCh switching capability loss
- Increased cross-talk
- Increased PMD/PDL

Fault Detectability (from a System Viewpoint)

- Loss of OCh output power (detected via LOS)
- Increased insertion loss (detected via EDC)
- Increased BER and cross-talk (?) (detected via EDC)

Comments

- In-out delay not uniform (varies per in-out connectivity)
- Currently, only small $N \times N$ switches ($N = 4$, $N = 32$) possible
- Insertion loss (~4 dB) per channel higher than other technologies
- Slow matrix switching speeds (several ms) lead to slow reconfiguration but few channels
- Requires beam polarization control (depending on LC technology)
- Requires operation conditions (temperature pressure?) control
- Small, compact, and inexpensive
- Device reliability must be understood

4.15 OADM: LiNbO₃ BASED

Function Entity. Wavelength distribution; OADM unit.

This component, at minimum, consists of a passive multiplexer, a demultiplexer, and LiNbO₃ switches. It can be integrated on one substrate or be assembled with individual parts. The components that are used in an OADM determine the parameters that could fail/degrade.

More complex OADMs may include MEMS array/matrix, filters, tunable array waveguide gratings, or other technologies not included in this phase.

Measurable Parameters	Degradable Parameters
OCh center wavelength	Not applicable
OCh width (line width)	Not applicable
Channel switching speed	Determined by manufacturer over the lifetime of component
Output optical power	Output power (per OCh)
Polarization	PMD per OCh (in picoseconds); polarization sensitivity (in fraction of a decibel); extinction ratio
Insertion loss per channel	Insertion loss (per OCh)
Switching speed per channel	Switching speed
Component temperature	Alters component parameters and thus cross-connected power and polarization state

Potential Faults	Impact
Faulty coupler	Loss of switching capability for several OChs; possible BER and cross-talk increase in other OChs
Temperature increase	Affects device parameters; possible phase shift, insertion loss per OCh

Fault Observability (Symptoms)

- OCh loss (one or more)
- OCh output power degradation
- OCh switching capability loss
- Increased cross-talk
- Increased PMD/PDL

Fault Detectability (from a System Viewpoint)

- Loss of OCh dropped (detected via LOS)
- Increased IL of OCh dropped (detected via EDC)
- Increased BER and cross-talk of OCh dropped (detected via EDC)
- Verification of added OCh frequency and power

Comments

- Not easy to implement large $N \times N$ OADM ($N = 64$?); needs testing strategy
- Requires verification of added OCh
- Requires verification strategy if dynamic allocation of OChs is supported
- Not easy to fault-manage large $N \times N$ switches on an OCh basis
- Protection switch possible but requires splitters
- Requires cross-talk control
- Requires PMD/PDL control
- Requires equalization
- May or may not use amplifiers

4.16 OADM: MEMS WITH GRATING

Function Entity.   Optical cross-connect, large compact optical fabrics, wavelength distribution (large OADM).

This component consists of a passive grating (for Mux and for Demux), passive optics (lens, 1/4-λ plate), circulators, and MEMS. Consequently, the parameters that could alter performance of an OADM and cause faults are the same as the MEMS and gratings. In addition, subcomponent alignment changes due to physical stresses (temperature, pressure, vibrations) and aging may result in further degradation of parameters.

Parameter degradation, fault mechanisms, and their impact on performance are dominated by gratings and MEMS (see corresponding entries above) as well as packaging.

4.17 TRANSMITTER: LASER

Function Entity.   Optical signal source, optical line cards, optical transponder unit.

Measurable Parameters	Degradable Parameters
Output power	Output power level
Wavelength (nm)	Center wavelength
Line width	Line width
Electrical-to-optical efficiency	Efficiency degradation affects output power
Tunability (tunable sources)	Tunability speed; wavelength range
Polarization of beam	Polarization of channel
Extinction ratio (dB)	Output power level
Stability	Wavelength and output power
Modulation depth (with integrated modulator)	Modulation depth (due to modulator degradation/fault)
Modulation rate [with integrated modulator (MHz, GHz)]	Rate degradation; spectral noise due to modulator electrical feedback
Component temperature	λ-shift; decrease of output power

Potential Faults	Impact
Output power loss	Loss of signal (at near end and far end); excessive ASE noise at far-end receiver (if OFA)
Wavelength drift	Degradation or loss of far-end received signal; S/N ratio decreases due to BER and/or cross-talk
Line-width broadening	Decreases optical power; increases BER and/or cross-talk
Modulation depth changes	BER due to inefficient demodulation; receiver ability to discriminate 0s and 1s
Tunability (tunable sources)	Potential packet loss; potential loss of signal/OCh
Temperature increase	Spectral output, laser parameters (power, λ_0, line width, etc.)

Fault Observability (Symptoms)

• Loss of laser output power at the transmitting end

• Laser output degradation (wavelength drift) due to bias and/or temperature variations

Fault Detectability (from a System Viewpoint)

- Loss of optical signal (detected via a mechanism at the laser)
- Output power degradation (detected via EDC)
- Wavelength shift (detected via EDC)
- Decreased S/N (detected via EDC)

Comments

- Lasers components (package) are complex modules that contain a large number of subcomponents to control the optical signal wavelength, line width, power level, temperature, and modulation parameters.
- Failure or degradation of any hidden subcomponent contributes to the overall laser component fault analysis.

4.18   RECEIVER: PIN DIODE

Function Entity.   Optical signal receiver, optical line cards, optical transponder unit.

Measurable Parameters	Degradable Parameters
Quantum efficiency	Degrades with aging; provided by manufacturer
Gain	Degrades with aging; affected by other parameters (voltage, current, temperature)
Output current	Related to quantum efficiency and gain
Response time	Related to time constant and quantum efficiency
Operating speed	Related to response time
Component temperature	Lowers quantum efficiency and gain; shifts λ-sensitivity

Potential Faults	Impact
Gain degradation	Signal integrity, increased BER
Speed degradation	Increased BER
Ceases to detect photons	Loss of incoming electrical signal
Dispersed receiving signal	Increased BER due to lower optical level of signal, crosstalk, jitter due to optical/electrical phase-locked loop (PLL), and BER due to S/N ratio decrease; possible loss of pointer (LOP) if power level below diode threshold
Temperature increase	Increased BER due to quantum efficiency decrease

Fault Observability (Symptoms)

- Loss of optical power per OCh within ($N = 4$?) periods at the receiving end declares loss of signal (LOS).

Fault Detectability (from a System Viewpoint)

- Loss of received optical signal (by one or more but not all receivers) terminating wavelengths within the fiber is detected via LOS detectors.
- If a LOP by all receivers is detected (and there is no electrical power loss at the receiver), then most likely the fiber is cut.

Comments

- A multiwavelength system is considered here.
- It may use an optical preamplification stage.
- PIN diode components (package) are complex modules that contain a large number of subcomponents, including filters and optical or electrical PLLs, to control the optical signal threshold, OCh wavelength, synchronization, temperature, and demodulation parameters.
- Failure or degradation of any hidden subcomponent contributes to the overall receiver component fault analysis.

4.19 FIBER: SINGLE MODE

Function Entity. Optical signal transmission medium. It is viewed as a key component in the optican network and in the system, as it affects the transmitter and the receiver.

Note: This section does not discriminate among various fiber types. It regards the fiber as a critical component that impacts the optical signal at the source and at the receiver as well as the performance of many optical components. The interaction of light with fiber becomes more pronounced in multiwavelength systems.

Measurable Parameters	Degradable Parameters
Length (L, km)	Signal power loss
Attenuation [$A(\lambda)$, dB/km]	Loss provided by manufacturer; by measuring power signal at input and at output
Material dispersion coefficient [$D_{mat}(\lambda)$, ps/nm-km]	Pulse spreading
Chromatic dispersion coefficient [$D_{chr}(\lambda)$, ps/nm-km]	Pulse spreading
Polarization mode (TE, TM)	Pulse spreading
Zero-dispersion wavelength (λ_0, nm)	Pulse spreading compensation
Birefringence	Power level and pulse spreading
Stress, bend, temperature	Propagation and dispersion parameters

Potential Faults	Impact
Fiber break	Loss of optical signal of all λs
Fiber stress	All propagation and dispersion characteristics; affects all or some OChs more than others
Fiber bend	All propagation and dispersion parameters; affects all or some OChs more than others

Fault Observability (Symptoms)

- Received optical power decreased
- Loss of received power

Detected Fault	Fault Correlation (from a System Viewpoint)
Loss of all signals	Fiber break; bad preamplifier OFA; bad OFA
Increased BER and cross-talk of some OChs	Stress on fiber; bad preamplifier OFA; bad OFA
Increased BER and cross-talk of all OChs	Stress on fiber; bad preamplifier OFA; bad OFA

Comments. System and networks fault management is required.

REFERENCES

[1] S. V. Kartalopoulos, *Introduction to DWDM: Data in a Rainbow,* IEEE Press, New York, 2000.

[2] S. V. Kartalopoulos, *Understanding SONET/SDH and ATM: Communications Networks for the next Millennium,* IEEE Press, New York, 1999.

[3] R. Ramaswami and K. N. Sivarajan, *Optical Networks,* Morgan Kaufmann, San Francisco, CA, 1998.

[4] B. Mukherjee, *Optical Communication Networks,* McGraw-Hill, New York, 1997.

[5] I. P. Kaminow, Ed., and T. L. Koch, Ed., *Optical Fiber Communications IIIA* and *Optical Fiber Communications IIIB,* Academic, New York, 1997.

[6] J. C. Palais, *Fiber Optic Communications,* 3rd ed., Prentice-Hall, Englewood Cliffs, NJ, 1992.

[7] R. G. Hunsperger, *Integrated Optics: Theory and Technology,* Springer-Verlag, New York, 1984.

[8] S. Sudo, Ed., *Optical Fiber Amplifiers: Materials, Devices, and Applications,* Artech House, Boston, 1997.

[9] J. Hecht, *The Laser Guidebook,* 2nd ed., Tab Books, Blue Ridge Summit, PA, 1992.

[10] T. Wildi, *Units and Conversion Charts,* 2nd ed., IEEE Press, New York, 1995.

[11] N. K. Dutta, "III–V Device Technologies for Lightwave Applications," *AT&T Tech. J.,* vol. 68, no. 1, 1989, pp. 5–18.

[12] J. J. Refi, "Optical Fibers for Optical Networking," *Bell Labs Tech. J.,* vol. 4, no. 1, 1999, pp. 246–261.

[13] R. J. Mears, L. Reekie, I. M. Jauncey, and D. N. Payne, "Low-Noise Erbium-Doped Fiber Amplifier Operating at 1.54 μm," *Electron. Lett.,* vol. 23, no. 19, 1987, pp. 1026–1028.

[14] E. Desurvire, J. R. Simpson, and P. C. Becker, "High-Gain Erbium-Doped Traveling-Wave Fiber Amplifiers," *Opt. Lett.,* vol. 12, no. 11, 1987, pp. 888–890.

[15] K-W. Cheung, "Acoustooptic Tunable Filters in Narrowband WDM Networks: System Issues and Network Applications," *IEEE JSAC,* vol. 8, no. 6, 1990, pp. 1015–1025.

[16] D. A. Smith, J. E. Baran, J. J. Johnson, and K-W. Cheung, "Integrated-Optic Acoustically-Tunable Filters for WDM Networks," *IEEE JSAC,* vol. 8, no. 6, 1990, pp. 1151–1159.

[17] S. R. Mallison, "Wavelength-Selective Filters for Single-Mode Fiber WDM Systems Using Fabry-Perot Interferometers," *Appl. Opt.,* vol 26, 1987, pp. 430–436.

[18] N. Goto and Y. Miyazaki, "Integrated Optical Multi-/Demultiplexer Using Acoustooptic Effect for Multiwavelength Optical Communications," *IEEE JSAC,* vol. 8, no. 6, 1990, pp. 1160–1168.

[19] N. Takato et al., "Silica-Based Integrated Optic Mach-Zehnder Multi/Demultiplexer Family with Channel Spacing of 0.01–250 nm," *IEEE JSAC,* vol. 8, no. 6, 1990, pp. 1120–1127.

[20] R. C. Alferness, "Waveguide Electro-Optic Modulators," *IEEE Trans. Microwave Theory Techn.,* vol. MTT-30, 1982, pp. 1121–1137.

[21] R. C. Alferness, "Guided-Wave Devices for Optical Communication," *IEEE J. Quant. Electron.*, vol. QE-17, 1981, pp. 946–949.

[22] R. C. Alferness and L. L. Buhl, "Low-Cross-Talk Waveguide Polarization Multiplexer/Demultiplexer for λ = 1.32 μm," *Opt. Lett.*, vol. 10, 1984, pp. 140–142.

[23] T. K. Findakly, "Glass Waveguides by Ion Exchange: A Review," *Opt. Eng.*, vol. 24, 1985, pp. 244–255.

[24] W. Warzanskyj, F. Heismann, and R. C. Alferness, "Polarization-Independent Electro-Acoustically Tunable Narrow-Band Wavelength Filter," *Appl. Phys. Lett.*, vol. 56, 1990, pp. 2009–2011.

[25] J. Frangen et al., "Integrated Optical, Acoustically-Tunable Wavelength Filter," *Proc. 6th European Conf. Integrated Opt.*, Paris, SPIE, 1989, post-deadline paper.

[26] F. Heismann, L. Buhl, and R. C. Alferness, "Electrooptically Tunable Narrowband Ti:LiNbO3 Wavelength Filter," *Electron. Lett.*, vol. 23, 1987, pp. 572–573.

[27] F. Ouellette, "All-Fiber for Efficient Dispersion Compensation," *Opt. Lett.*, vol. 16, no. 5, 1991, pp. 303–304.

[28] R. M. Measures, A. T. Alavie, M. LeBlanc, S. Huang, M. Ohn, R. Masskant, and D. Graham, "Controlled Grating Chirp for Variable Optical Dispersion Compensation," *Proceedings, 13th Annual Conference on European Fiber Optic Communications and Networks,* Brighton, England, 1995, pp. 38–41.

[29] G. D. Boyd and F. Heismann, "Tunable Acoustooptic Reflection Filters in LiNbO3 without a Doppler Shift," *J. Lightwave Technol.*, vol. 7, 1989, pp. 625–631.

[30] L. G. Kazovsky, "Optical Signal Processing for Lightwave Communications Networks," *IEEE JSAC,* vol. 8, no. 6, 1990, pp. 973–982.

[31] S. E. Miller, "Coupled-Wave Theory and Waveguide Applications," *Bell Syst. Tech. J.,* vol. 33, 1954, pp. 661–719.

[32] A. Yariv, "Coupled Mode Theory for Guided Wave Optics," *IEEE J. Quant. Electron.,* vol. QE-9, 1973, pp. 919–933.

[33] D. Sadot and E. Boimovich, "Tunable Optical Filters for Dense WDM Networks," *IEEE Commun. Mag.,* vol. 36, no. 12, 1998, pp. 50–55.

[34] M. Zirngibl, "Multifrequency Lasers and Applications in WDM Networks," *IEEE Commun. Mag.,* vol. 36, no. 12, 1998, pp. 39–41.

[35] S. D. Personick, "Receiver Design for Digital Fiber Optic Communication Systems, I," *Bell Syst. Tech. J.,* vol. 52, no. 6, 1973, pp. 843–874.

[36] S. D. Personick, "Receiver Design for Digital Fiber Optic Communication Systems, II," *Bell Syst. Tech. J.,* vol. 52, no. 6, 1973, pp. 875–886.

[37] F. Tong, "Multiwavelength Receivers for WDM Systems," *IEEE Commun. Mag.,* vol. 36, no. 12, 1998, pp. 42–49.

[38] K. A. McGreer, "Arrayed Waveguide Grating for Wavelength Routing," *IEEE Commun. Mag.,* vol. 36, no. 12, 1998, pp. 62–68.

[39] A. Iocco, H. G. Limberger, and R. P. Salathe, "Bragg Grating Fast Tunable Filter," *Electron. Lett.,* vol. 33, no. 25, 1997, pp. 2147–2148.

[40] M. K. Smit and C. van Dam, "PHASAR-Based WDM-Devices: Principles, Design and Application," *IEEE J. Sel. Topics Quant. Electron.,* vol. 2, no. 2, 1996, pp. 236–250.

[41] H. Tanobe et al, "Temperature Insensitive Arrayed Waveguide Gratings on InP Substrate," *IEEE Photon Tech. Lett.*, vol. 10, no. 2, 1998, pp. 235–237.

[42] D. Nesset, T. Kelly, and D. Marcenac, "All-Optical Wavelength Conversion Using SOA Nonlinearities," *IEEE Commun. Mag.*, vol. 36, no. 12, 1998, pp. 56–61.

[43] J. M. Senior and S. D. Cusworth, "Devices for Wavelength Multiplexing and Demultiplexing," *IEE Proc.*, vol. 136, no. 3, 1989, pp. 183–202.

[44] Y. K. Chen and C. C. Lee, "Fiber Bragg Grating-Based Large Nonblocking Multiwavelength Cross-Connects," *J. Lightwave Technol.*, vol. 16, no. 10, 1998, pp. 1746–1756.

[45] C. R. Doerr, "Proposed WDM Cross Connect Using a Planar Arrangement of Waveguide Grating Routers and Phase Shifters," *IEEE Photon. Technol. Lett.*, vol. 10, 1998, pp. 528–530.

[46] J. E. Ford, V. A. Aksyuk, D. J. Bishop, and J. A. Walker, "Wavelength Add/Drop Switching Using Tilting Micromirrors," *J. Lightwave Technol.*, vol. 17, no. 5, 1999, pp. 904–911.

[47] J. R. Thompson and R. Roy, "Multiple Four-Wave Mixing Process in an Optical Fiber," *Opt. Lett.*, vol. 16, no. 8, 1991, pp. 557–559.

[48] K. Inoue, "Experimental Study on Channel Crosstalk Due to Fiber Four-Wave Mixing around the Zero-Dispersion Wavelength," *IEEE J. Lighwave Technol.*, vol. LT-12, no. 6, 1994, pp. 1023–1028.

[49] C. A. Brackett, "Dense Wavelength Division Multiplexing Networks: Principles and Applications," *IEEE JSAC*, vol. 8, no. 6, 1990, pp. 948–964.

[50] C. R. Giles and M. Spector, "The Wavelength Add/Drop Multiplexer for Lightwave Communication Networks," *Bell Labs Tech. J.*, vol. 4, no. 1, 1999, pp. 207–229.

[51] U. Koren et al., "Wavelength Division Multiplexing Light Sources with Integrated Quantum Well Tunable Lasers and Optical Amplification," *Appl. Phys. Lett.*, vol. 54, 1989, pp. 2056–2058.

[52] G. Coquin, K. W. Cheung, and M. Choy, "Single- and Multiple-Wavelength Operation of Acousto-Optically Tuned Lasers at 1.3 Microns," *Proc. 11th IEEE Int. Semiconductor Laser Conf.*, Boston, 1988, pp. 130–131.

[53] H. Kobrinski and K. W. Cheung, "Wavelength-Tunable Optical Filters: Applications and Technologies," *IEEE Commun. Mag.*, vol. 27, 1989, pp. 53–63.

[54] S. Suzuki et al., "A Photonic Wavelength-Division Switching System Using Tunable Laser Diode Filters," *ICC '89 Conference Records*, Boston, 1989, paper 23.1.

[55] C. Dragone, "Efficient $N \times N$ Star Couplers Using Fourier Optics," *J. Lightwave Technol.*, vol. 7, 1989, pp. 479–489.

[56] C. M. Ragdale, D. Reid, D. J. Robbins, and J. Buus, "Narrowband Fiber Grating Filters," *IEEE JSAC*, vol. 8, no. 6, 1990, pp. 1146–1150.

[57] Y. Sun, A. K. Srivastava, J. Zhou, and J. W. Sulhoff, "Optical Fiber Amplifiers for WDM Optical Networks," *Bell Labs Tech. J.*, vol. 4, no. 1, 1999, pp. 187–206.

[58] M. J. Adams, "Theory of Twin-Guide Fabry-Perot Laser Amplifiers," *IEE Proc.*, vol. 136, no. 5, 1989, pp. 287–292.

[59] G. J. Cannell, A. Robertson, and R. Worthington, "Practical Realization of a High Density Diode-Coupled Wavelength Demultiplexer," *IEEE JSAC*, vol. 8, no. 6, 1990, pp. 1141–1145.

[60] A. J. Lowery, "Computer-Aided Photonics Design," *IEEE Spectrum*, vol. 34, no. 4, 1997, pp. 26–31.

[61] K. S. Giboney, L. A. Aronson, and B. E. Lemoff, "The Ideal Light Source for Datanets," *IEEE Spectrum*, vol. 35, no. 2, 1998, pp. 43–53.

[62] M-C. Amann and W. Thulke, "Continuously Tunable Laser Diodes: Longitudinal versus Transverse Tuning Scheme," *IEEE JSAC*, vol. 8, no. 6, 1990, pp. 1169–1177.

[63] K. Kobayashi and I. Mito, "Single Frequency and Tunable Laser Diodes," *J. Lightwave Technol.*, vol 6, 1988, pp. 1623–1633.

[64] L. A. Coldren and S. W. Corzine, "Continuously Tunable Single Frequency Semiconductor Lasers," *IEEE J. Quantum Electron.*, vol. QE-23, 1987, pp. 903–908.

[65] M. Okuda and K. Onaka, "Tunability of Distributed Bragg Reflector Laser by Modulating Refractive Index in Corrugated Waveguide," *Jpn. J. Appl. Phys.*, vol. 16, 1977, pp. 1501–1502.

[66] Y. Kotaki, M. Matsuda, H. Ishikawa, and H. Imai, "Tunable DBR Laser with Wide Tuning Range," *Electron. Lett.*, vol. 24, 1988, pp. 503–505.

[67] H. A. Haus, *Waves and Fields in Optoelectronics*, Prentice-Hall, Englewood Cliffs, NJ, 1984.

[68] S. Adachi, "Refractive Indices of III–IV Compounds: Key Properties of InGaAsP Relevant to Device Design," *J. Appl. Phys.*, vol. 53, 1982, pp. 5863–5869.

[69] J. Stone and D. Marcuse, "Ultrahigh Finesse Fiber Fabry-Perot Interferometers," *J. Lightwave Technol.*, vol. LT-4, no. 4, 1986, pp. 382–385.

[70] A. A. M. Saleh and J. Stone, "Two-Stage Fabry-Perot Filters as Demultiplexers in Optical FDMA LAN's," *J. Lightwave Technol.*, vol. LT-7, 1989, pp. 323–330.

[71] S. R. Mallinson, "Wavelength Selective Filters for Single-Mode Fiber WDM Systems Using Fabry-Perot Interferometers," *Appl. Opt.*, vol. 26, 1987, pp. 430–436.

[72] A. M. Hill and D. B. Payne, "Linear Crosstalk in Wavelength Division Multiplexed Optical Fiber Transmission Systems," *J. Lightwave Technol.*, vol. LT-3, 1985, pp. 643–651.

[73] G. Hernandez, *Fabry-Perot Interferometers*, Cambridge University Press, Cambridge, 1986.

[74] F. J. Leonberger, "Applications of Guided-Wave Interferometers," *Laser Focus*, Mar. 1982, pp. 125–129.

[75] H. Van de Stadt and J. M. Muller, "Multimirror Fabry-Perot Interferometers," *J. Opt. Soc. Am. A*, vol. 2, 1985, pp. 1363–1370.

[76] P. A. Humblet and W. M. Hamdy, "Crosstalk Analysis and Filter Optimization of Single- and Double-Cavity Fabry-Perot Filters," *IEEE JSAC*, vol. 8, no. 6, 1990, pp. 1095–1107.

[77] K. Y. Eng, M. A. Santoro, T. L. Koch, J. Stone, and W. W. Snell, "Star-Coupler-Based Optical Cross-Connect Switch Experiments with Tunable Receivers," *IEEE JSAC*, vol. 8, no. 6, 1990, pp. 1026–1031.

[78] H. Toba, K. Oda, K. Nosu, and N. Takato, "Factors Affecting the Design of Optical FDM Information Distribution Systems," *IEEE JSAC*, vol. 8, no. 6, 1990, pp. 965–972.

[79] H. Onaka, et al., "1.1 Tb/s WDM Transmission Over a 150 Km 1.3 Zero-Dispersion Single-Mode Fiber," *OFC '96*, San Jose, CA, Feb. 1996, pp. PD19:1–5.

[80] A. R. Chraplyvy, "Optical Power Limits in Multi-Channel Wavelength-Division-Multiplexed System due to Stimulated Raman Scattering," *Electron. Lett.,* vol. 20, no. 2, 1984, pp. 58–59.

[81] K. Inoue, "Four-Wave Mixing in an Optical Fiber in the Zero-Dispersion Wavelength Region," *IEEE J. Lightwave Technol.,* vol. LT-10, no. 11, 1992, pp. 1553–1563.

[82] K. Inoue, "Suppression of Fiber Four-Wave Mixing in Multichannel Transmission Using Birefringent Elements," *IEICE Trans. Commun.,* vol. E76-B, no. 9, 1993, pp. 1219–1221.

[83] K. Nosu, *Optical FDM Network Technologies,* Artech House, Boston, 1997.

[84] M. Cvijetic, *Coherent and Nonlinear Lightwave Communications,* Artech House, Boston, 1996.

[85] H. Toba and K. Nosu, "Optical Frequency Division Multiplexing System—Review of Key Technologies and Applications," *IEICE Trans. Commun.,* vol. E75-B, no. 4, 1992, pp. 243–255.

[86] D. Cotter, "Stimulated Brillouin Scattering in Monomode Optical Fiber," *J. Opt. Commun.,* vol. 4, 1983, pp. 10–16.

[87] P. S. Henry, "Lightwave Primer," *IEEE J. Quant. Electron.,* vol. QE-21, 1985, pp. 1862–1879.

[88] M. Kawasaki, "Silica Waveguides on Silicon and Their Application to Integrated Optic Components," *Opt. Quant. Electron.,* vol. 22, 1990, pp. 391–416.

[89] L. Kazovsky, S. Benedetto, and A. Willner, *Optical Fiber Communication Systems,* Artech House, Boston, 1996.

[90] N. A. Jackman, S. H. Patel, B. P. Mikkelsen, and S. K. Korotky, "Optical Cross Connect for Optical Networking," *Bell Labs Tech. J.,* vol. 4, no. 1, 1999, pp. 262–281.

[91] H. Takahashi et al., "Arrayed-Waveguide Grating for Wavelength Division Multiplexing/Demultiplexing with Nanometer Resolution," *Electron. Lett.,* vol. 26, 1990, pp. 87–88.

[92] J. Minowa and Y. Fujii, "Dielectric Multilayer Thin Film Filters for WDM Transmission," *IEEE J. Lightwave Technol.,* vol. 1, no. 1, 1983, pp. 116–121.

[93] W. K. Chen, *Passive and Active Filters,* Wiley, New York, 1986.

[94] R. Watanabe et al., "Optical Multi/Demultiplexers for Single-Mode Fiber Transmission," *IEEE J. Quant. Electron.,* vol. 17, no. 6, 1981, pp. 947–951.

[95] Y. Hibino et al., "High Reliability Silica Based PLC 1X8 Splitters on Si," *Electron. Lett.,* vol. 30, no. 8, 1994, pp. 640–641.

[96] K. Kato et al., "Packaging of Large-Scale Integrated Optic $N \times N$ Star Couplers," *IEEE Photon. Technol. Lett.,* vol. 4, no. 33, 1993, pp. 348–351.

[97] H. Rokugawa et al., "Wavelength Conversion Laser Diodes Application to Wavelength-Division Photonic Cross-Connect Node with Multistage Configuration," *IEICE Trans. Commun.,* vol. E-75-B, no. 4, 1992, pp. 267–273.

[98] O. Ishida and H. Toba, "A 1.55-mm Lightwave Frequency Synthesizer," *IEICE Trans. Commun.,* vol. E75-B, no. 4, 1992, pp. 275–280.

[99] K. Vilhelmsson, "Simultaneous Forward and Backward Raman Scattering in Low-Attenuation Single-Mode Fibers," *J. Lightwave Technol.,* vol. LT-4, no. 4, 1986, pp. 400–404.

[100] H. Kobrinski and K-W. Cheung, "Wavelength-Tunable Optical Filters: Applications and Technologies," *IEEE Commun. Mag.*, Oct. 1989, pp. 53–63.

[101] R. Tewari and K. Thyagarajan, "Analysis of Tunable Single-Mode Fiber Directional Couplers Using Simple and Accurate Relations," *J. Lightwave Technol.*, vol. LT-4, no. 4, 1986, pp. 386–399.

[102] N. Kashima, *Passive Optical Components for Optical Fiber Transmission*, Artech House, Boston, 1995.

[103] S. Kawakami, "Light Propagation along Periodic Metal-Dielectric Layers," *Appl. Opt.*, vol. 22, 1983, p. 2426.

[104] K. Shiraishi, S. Sugayama, K. Baba, and S. Kawakami, "Microisolator," *Appl. Opt.*, vol. 25, 1986, p. 311.

[105] K. Shiraishi, S. Sugayama, and S. Kawakami, "Fiber Faraday Rotator," *Appl. Opt.*, vol. 23, 1984, p. 1103.

[106] W. Eickhoff, "In-Line Fiber-Optic Polarizer," *Electron. Lett.*, vol. 6, 1980, p. 762.

[107] T. Hosaka, K. Okamoto, and J. Noda, "Single-Mode Fiber Type Polarizer," *IEEE J. Quant. Electron.*, vol. QE-18, 1982, p. 1569.

[108] R. A. Bergh, H. C. Lefevre, and H. J. Shaw, "Single-Mode Fiber-Optic Polarizer," *Opt. Lett.*, vol. 5, 1980, p. 479.

[109] J. C. Palais, *Fiber Optic Communications*, 3rd ed., Prentice-Hall, Englewood Cliffs, NJ, 1992.

[110] M. Francon, *Optique: formation et traitment des images*, Macon & Cie, Paris, 1972.

[111] T. G. Robertazzi, Ed., *Performance Evaluation of High Speed Switching Fabrics and Networks*, IEEE Press, New York, 1993.

[112] Y. Pan, C. Qiao, and Y. Yang, "Optical Multistage Interconnection Networks: New Challenges and Approaches," *IEEE Commun. Mag.*, vol. 37, no. 2, 1999, pp. 50–56.

[113] J. G. Eden, "Photochemical Processing of Semiconductors: New Applications for Visible and Ultraviolet Lasers," *IEEE Circuits Devices Mag.*, vol. 2, no. 1, 1986, pp. 18–24.

[114] R. J. von Gutfeld, "Laser-Enhanced Plating and Etching for Microelectronic Applications," *IEEE Circuits Devices Mag.*, vol. 2, no. 1, 1986, pp. 57–60.

[115] J. Bokor, A. R. Neureuther, and W. G. Oldham, "Advanced Lithography for ULSI," *IEEE Circuits Devices Mag.*, vol. 12, no. 1, 1996, pp. 11–15.

[116] A. Yariv, "Quantum Well Semiconductor Lasers Are Taking Over," *IEEE Circuits Devices Mag.*, vol. 5, no. 6, 1989, pp. 25–28.

[117] J. LaCourse, "Laser Primer for Fiber-Optics Users," *IEEE Circuits Devices Mag.*, vol. 8, no. 2, 1992, pp. 27–32.

[118] Z. V. Nesterova and I. V. Aleksaandrov, "Optical-Fiber Sources of Coherent Light," *Sov. J. Opt. Technol.*, vol 54, no. 3, 1987, pp. 183–190.

[119] T. Komukai et al., "Upconversion Pumped Thulium-Doped Fluoride Fiber Amplifier and Laser Operating at 1.47 μm," *IEEE Quant. Electron.*, vol. 31, 1995, pp. 1880–1889.

[120] G. Eisenstein, "Semiconductor Optical Amplifiers," *IEEE Circuits Devices Mag.*, vol. 5, no. 4, 1989, pp. 25–30.

[121] C. F. Buhrer, "Four Waveplate Dual Tuner for Birefringent Filters and Multiplexers," *Appl. Opt.*, vol. 26, no. 17, 1987, pp. 3628–3632.

[122] J. W. Evans, "The Birefringent Filter," *J. Opt. Soc. Am.,* vol. 39, 1949, p. 229.

[123] H. Hinton, *An Introduction to Photonic Switching Fabrics,* Plenum, New York, 1993.

[124] C. Tocci and H. J. Caufield, *Optical Interconnection—Foundations and Applications,* Artech House, Boston, 1994.

[125] A. Budman et al., "Multi-Gigabit Optical Packet Switch for Self-Routing Networks with Subcarrier Addressing," *Proc. OFC '92,* San Jose, CA, Feb. 1992, paper Tu04.

[126] C-K. Chan, L-K. Chen, and K-W. Cheung, "A Fast Channel-Tunable Optical Transmitter for Ultrahigh-Speed All-Optical Time-Division Multi-Access Network," *IEEE JSAC,* vol. 14, no. 5, 1996, pp. 1052–1056.

[127] K. Padmanabhan and A. N. Netravali, "Dilated Networks for Photonic Switching," *IEEE Trans. Commun.,* vol. 35, no. 12, 1987, pp. 1357–1365.

[128] C. Qiao et al., "A Time Domain Approach for Avoiding Crosstalk in Optical Blocking Multistage Interconnection Networks," *J. Lightwave Technol.,* vol. 12, no. 10, 1994, pp. 1854–1862.

[129] R. A. Thompson, "The Dilated Slipped Banyan Switching Network Architecture for Use in an All-Optical Local-Area Network," *J. Lightwave Technol.,* vol. 9, no. 12, 1991, pp. 1780–1787.

[130] D. Hunter and D. Smith, "New Architecture for Optical TDM Switching," *J. Lightwave Technol.,* vol. 11, no. 3, 1993, pp. 495–511.

[131] E. Nussbaum, "Communication Network Needs and Technologies—A Place for Photonic Switching," *IEEE JSAC,* vol. 6, no. 7, 1988, pp. 1036–1043.

[132] S. A. Cassidy and P. Yennadhiou, "Optimum Switching Architectures Using D-Fiber Optical Space Switches," *IEEE JSAC,* vol. 6, no. 7, 1988, pp. 1044–1051.

[133] C. J. Smith, "Nonblocking Photonic Switch Networks," *IEEE JSAC,* vol. 6, no. 7, 1988, pp. 1052–1062.

[134] J. D. Evankow, Jr. and R. A. Thompson, "Photonic Switching Modules Designed with Laser Diode Amplifiers," *IEEE JSAC,* vol. 6, no. 7, 1988, pp. 1087–1095.

[135] W. D. Johnston, Jr., M. A. DiGiuseppe, and D. P. Wilt, "Liquid and Vapor Phase Growth of III–V Materials for Photonic Devices," *AT&T Tech. J.,* vol. 68, no. 1, 1989, pp. 53–63.

[136] W. G. Dautremont-Smith, R. J. McCoy, and R. H. Burton, "Fabrication Technologies for III–V Compound Semiconductor Photonic and Electronic Devices," *AT&T Tech. J.,* vol. 68, no. 1, 1989, pp. 64–82.

[137] N. K. Dutta, "III–V Device Technologies for Lightwave Applications," *AT&T Tech. J.,* vol. 68, no. 1, 1989, pp. 5–18.

[138] K. Y. Eng, "A Photonic Knockout Switch for High-Speed Packet Networks," *IEEE JSAC,* vol. 6, no. 7, 1988, pp. 1107–1116.

[139] R. C. Alferness, "Waveguide Electrooptic Switch Arrays," *IEEE JSAC,* vol. 6, no. 7, 1988, pp. 1117–1130.

[140] T. Ikegami and H. Kawaguchi, "Semiconductor Devices in Photonic Switching," *IEEE JSAC,* vol. 6, no. 7, 1988, pp. 1131–1140.

[141] R. I. Macdonald, "Terminology for Photonic Matrix Switches," *IEEE JSAC,* vol. 6, no. 7, 1988, pp. 1141–1151.

[142] J. V. Wright, S. R. Mallinson, and C. A. Millar, "A Fiber-Based Crosspoint Switch Using High-Refractive Index Interlay Materials," *IEEE JSAC,* vol. 6, no. 7, 1988, pp. 1160–1168.

[143] J. Skinner and C. H. R. Lane, "A Low-Crosstalk Microoptic Liquid Crystal Switch," *IEEE JSAC,* vol. 6, no. 7, 1988, pp. 1178–1185.

[144] T. Morioka and M. Saruwatari, "Ultrafast All-Optical Switching Utilizing the Optical Kerr Effect in Polarization-Maintaining Single-Mode Fibers," *IEEE JSAC,* vol. 6, no. 7, 1988, pp. 1186–1198.

[145] H. S. Hinton, "Architectural Considerations for Photonic Switching Networks," *IEEE JSAC,* vol. 6, no. 7, 1988, pp. 1209–1226.

[146] H. Inoue, H. Nakamura, K. Morosawa, Y. Sasaki, T. Katsuyama, and N. Chinone, "An 8 mm Length Nonblocking 4 × 4 Optical Switch Array," *IEEE JSAC,* vol. 6, no. 7, 1988, pp. 1262–1266.

[147] R. Driggers, P. Cox, and T. Edwards, *An Introduction to Infrared and Electro-Optical Systems,* Artech House, Boston, 1999.

[148] R. Marz, *Integrated Optics: Design and Modeling,* Artech House, Boston, 1995.

[149] J. Hecht, *Understanding Fiber Optics,* Prentice-Hall, Englewood Cliffs, NJ, 1999.

[150] S. V. Kartalopoulos, "A Plateau of Performance?" Guest Editorial, *IEEE Commun. Mag.,* Sept. 1992, pp. 13–14.

[151] J. Nellist, *Understanding Telecommunications and Lightwave Systems,* IEEE Press, New York, 1996.

[152] W. Y. Zhou and Y. Wu, "COFDM: An Overview," *IEEE Trans. Broadcasting,* vol. 41, no. 1, 1995, pp. 1–8.

[153] D. J. Bishop and V. A. Aksyuk, "Optical MEMS Answer High-Speed Networking Requirements," *Electron. Design,* Apr. 5, 1999, pp. 85–92.

[154] R. Tewari and K. Thyagarajan, "Analysis of Tunable Single-Mode Fiber Directional Couplers Using Simple and Accurate Relations," *IEEE J. Lightwave Technol.,* vol. LT-4, no. 4, 1986, pp. 386–390.

[155] N. A. Olsson and J. Hegarty, "Noise Properties of a Raman Amplifier," *IEEE J. Lightwave Technol.,* vol. LT-4, no. 4, 1986, pp. 396–399.

[156] N. Shibata, K. Nosu, K. Iwashita, and Y. Azuma, "Transmission Limitations Due to Fiber Nonlinearities in Optical FDM Systems," *IEEE J. Selected Areas Commun.,* vol. 8, no. 6, 1990, pp. 1068–1077.

[157] A. Brauer and P. Dannberg, "Polymers for Passive and Switching Waveguide Components for Optical Communication," in *Polymers in Optics: Physics, Chemistry, and Applications,* R. A. Lessard and W. F. Frank, Eds., SPIE, Bellingham, WA, 1996, pp. 334–348.

[158] J. M. Zavada, "Optical Modulation in Photonic Circuits," in *Photonic Devices and Systems,* R. C. Hunsperver, Ed., Marcel Dekker, New York, 1994, pp. 61–92.

STANDARDS

[1] ANSI/IEEE 812–1984, "Definition of Terms Relating to Fiber Optics," 1984.

[2] ITU-T Recommendation G.650, "Definition and Test Methods for the Relevant Parameters of Single-Mode Fibres," 1996.

[3] ITU-T Recommendation G.652, version 4, "Characteristics of a Single-Mode Optical Fiber Cable," Apr. 1997.

[4] ITU-T Recommendation G.653, version 4, "Characteristics of a Dispersion-Shifted Single-Mode Optical Fiber Cable," Apr. 1997.

[5] ITU-T Recommendation G.655, version 10, "Characteristics of a Non-Zero Dispersion-Shifted Single-Mode Optical Fiber Cable," Oct. 1996.

[6] ITU-T Recommendation G.661, "Definition and Test Methods for the Relevant Generic Parameters of Optical Fiber Amplifiers," Nov. 1996.

[7] ITU-T Recommendation G.662, "Generic Characteristics of Optical Fiber Amplifier Devices and Sub-Systems," July 1995.

[8] ITU-T Recommendation G.663, "Application Related Aspects of Optical Fiber Amplifier Devices and Sub-Systems," July 1995.

[9] ITU-T Recommendation G.671, "Transmission Characteristics of Passive Optical Components," Nov. 1996.

[10] ITU-T Recommendation G.821, "Error Performance of an International Digital Connection Operating at a Bit Rate below the Primary Rate and Forming Part of an Integrated Services Digital Network," Aug. 1996.

[11] ITU-T Recommendation G.826, "Error Performance Parameters and Objectives for International, Constant Bit Rate Digital Paths at or above the Primary Rate," Feb. 1999.

[12] ITU-T Recommendation G.828, "Error Performance Parameters and Objectives for International, Constant Bit Rate Synchronous Digital Paths," Feb. 2000.

[13] ITU-T Recommendation G.911, "Parameters and Calculation Methodologies for Reliability and Availability of Fibre Optic Systems," 1997.

[14] Go to http://www.itu.int/ITU-T/index.html for a list of ITU standards.

[15] Telcordia GR-63-CORE, "Network Equipment Building System (NEBS)—Generic Equipment Requirements," Oct. 1995.

[16] Telcordia GR-1221-CORE, "Generic Reliability Assurance Requirements for Fiber Optic Branching Components," Jan. 1999.

[17] Bellcore, TR-NWT-233, "Digital Cross Connect System," Nov. 1992.

[18] Telcordia TR-NWT-000468, "Reliability Assurance Practices for Optoelectronic Devices in Central Office Applications," Dec. 1998.

[19] Telcordia TR-NWT-917, "Regenerator," Oct. 1990.

CHAPTER 5

FAULT CORRELATION

5.1 INTRODUCTION

In this chapter, we examine the detectable degradations/faults and correlate them by component parameter change. Correlation of faults and component parameter changes are grouped by component type.

5.2 CORRELATION OF FAULTS AND COMPONENT PARAMETER CHANGES

OCh Power Degradation Due To

- Laser launched optical power loss
- Laser wavelength drift due to parametric changes
- Modulator failure
- Loss of tunability (tunable sources, receivers and filters)
- Tunability error (tunable sources, receivers and filters)
- OFA pump wavelength drift
- OFA pump gain degraded or lost
- OFA directional coupler malfunctioning
- SOA injection current changed
- SOA coupling inefficiency
- SOA temperature increase
- Diode receiver failure
- Loss of optical phase-locked loop (OPLL)

- Excessive IL per OCh due to component temperature variation
- OADM failure to add or drop OCh
- Mux/Demux excessive line-width spread/OCh power decrease
- Mux/Demux faulty coupler
- Mux/Demux polarization rotated (polarization-sensitive device/receiver)
- Mirror (MEMS) does not rest at correct position
- Loss of OCh switching capability due to faulty mirror (MEMS stuck at fault)
- Loss of switching capability of OChs due to coupler fault
- Fiber cut or fiber disconnected

Loss of Electrical Signal (after Diode)

- Diode ceases to detect photons
- Demodulator failure
- Loss of clock circuitry

Passed the diode, information is in the electronic regime and signal integrity is monitored using in-service traditional methods.

This is considered a fault in devices that have to operate within a very narrow temperature window and thus may be temperature stabilized.

Loss of Clock Due To

- Loss of OCh power

Component Temperature Change

- Degrades component parameters that cause deviation from operating conditions and, depending on component, may cause optical signal in wavelength, output power, and/or S/N

Increased BER and Cross-Talk Due To

- OCh wavelength shift
- OCh phase shift increase
- OCh polarization change
- OCh dispersion increase
- OCh IL increase

- Launched optical power decrease
- Received optical power decrease
- Line-width broadening [due to group delay (GD), differential GD (DGD), PMD, or chromatic dispersion (CD)]
- Line-width broadening (due to OA, Mux/Demux, filter)
- Line-width broadening due to laser temperature
- Directional coupler parametric changes
- Excessive dispersion accumulation
- Faulty mirror (MEMS stuck at faulty position)
- Mirror (MEMS) does not rest at correct position
- Mirror (MEMS) vibrations
- Laser wavelength drift/broadening due to temperature or tunability
- Mux/Demux λ discrimination disabled
- Mux/Demux polarization change (polarization-sensitive device/receiver)
- Phase shift by Mux/Demux due to temperature increase
- IL per OCh by Mux/Demux due to temperature increase
- OFA high power causes nonlinearities on certain λs
- OFA pump power degrades
- OFA pump inoperable
- OFA pump wavelength drift (gain degradation of certain λs)
- OFA coupler malfunctioning
- Increased ASE noise due to OFA
- Increased cumulative ASE
- OFA gain of an OCh decreases more than others due to misequalization
- Amplification gain of OFA or SOA decrease
- PDL increase (due to SOA temperature increase)
- SOA coupling inefficiency
- SOA gain decrease
- SOA injection current change
- Modulation depth decrease (due to laser/modulator parametric changes)
- Inefficient demodulation (causes receiver inability to discriminate 0s and 1s)
- Receiving diode gain degrades (due to parametric changes)
- Receiving diode quantum efficiency degrades (due to parametric change)

- Filter [Fabry-Perot (FP)] parametric variations (due to temperature, stress, or field changes)
- Passband IL (per OCh) caused by FP (due to parametric changes)
- Filter (Bragg) detuning (due to dispersion per OCh)
- Filter (Bragg) parametric variations (due to temperature or stress changes)
- Filter (AOTF) detuning (due to parametric changes)
- Filter (AOTF) detuning (due to RF shift)
- Filter (AOTF) polarization change*
- Filter (AOTF) λ registration mismatch (due to Doppler) frequency shift*
- Increased PDL [due to (AOF) filter RF power change]
- Increased PDL (due to filter parametric changes)
- Coupling loss (due to filter misalignment of polarization state)
- OCh dispersion increase (caused by temperature, stress, or field variation)
- Power amplitude of λ_o decrease (due to a component IL increase)
- Nonlinear interaction of two OChs (due to channel spacing decrease)

5.3   OPEN ISSUES: NONLINEAR EFFECTS

Dispersion and nonlinear phenomena impact BER and cross-talk levels. They are not readily and directly detected. Thus, a better mechanism is needed to distinguish among the many sources of BER and cross-talk for faster fault identification and localization.

Self-modulation or modulation instability is a phenomenon that degrades the width of the pulse when the center wavelength is in the anomalous dispersion regime (above the zero-dispersion wavelength). This phenomenon needs to be further understood as it impacts the received BER and cross-talk.

FWM is more intense at the near end of the fiber and is expected to fade out as the OChs are attenuated (after 20–50 km). FWM could be diminished if OChs were synchronized. Reducing FWM improves the BER at the receiver, which effectively may increase the fiber span. Synchronization methods need be investigated and the improvement quantified.

ITU-T has defined center frequencies evenly spaced (100 and 50 GHz). Proposals have been made to space them unevenly to minimize FWM. However, evenly

---

*Not applicable in all implementations

spaced frequencies allow for linear expansion of OChs and better dynamic wavelength allocation and management. This needs to be further studied and understood so that faults related to nonlinearities are minimized.

Fiber amplifiers with rare-earth dopants need to be further investigated. It would be advantageous if a single OFA could be used for the complete spectrum 1.3–1.6 μm. This would also simplify failure detection mechanisms and actions.

PMD is an area that needs further investigation.

Integration of optical components (some using nonlinearities) is an emerging area with great potential. This may impact favorably the fault analysis process.

REFERENCES

[1] S. V. Kartalopoulos, *Introduction to DWDM Technology: Data in a Rainbow,* IEEE Press, New York, 2000.

[2] S. V. Kartalopoulos, *Understanding SONET/SDH and ATM: Networks for the Next Millennium,* IEEE Press, New York, 1999.

[3] S. V. Kartalopoulos, "Aspects in Fault Detectability," *Proceedings of ACM'2000,* London, Nov. 14–16, 2000, to be published.

[4] B. Furht, *Handbook of Internet and Multimedia: Systems and Applications,* IEEE Press, New York, 1999.

[5] L. G. Raman, *Fundamentals of Telecommunications Network Management,* IEEE Press, New York, 1999.

[6] A. Borella, G. Cancellieri, and F. Chiaraluce, *Wavelength Division Multiple Access Optical Networks,* Artech House, Boston, 1998.

[7] B. T. Doshi, S. Dravida, P. Harshavardhana, O. Hauser, and Y. Wang, "Optical Network Design and Restoration," *Bell Labs Tech. J.,* vol. 4, no. 1, 1999, pp. 58–84.

[8] S. Chatterjee and S. Pawlowski, "All-Optical Networks," *Commun. ACM,* vol. 47, no. 6, 1999, pp. 74–83.

[9] S. V. Kartalopoulos, "A Manhattan Fiber Distributed Data Interface Architecture," in *Proceedings of IEEE Globecom'90,* San Diego, Dec. 2–5, 1990.

[10] S. V. Kartalopoulos, "Disaster Avoidance in the Manhattan Fiber Distributed Data Interface Network," in *Proceedings of IEEE Globecom'93,* Houston, TX, Dec. 2, 1993.

[11] S. R. Johnson and V. L. Nichols, "Advanced Optical Networking—Lucent's MONET Network Elements," *Bell Labs Tech. J.,* vol. 4, no. 1, 1999, pp. 145–162.

[12] Y. Chen, M. T. Fatehi, H. J. LaRoche, J. Z. Larsen, and B. L. Nelson, "Metro Optical Networking," *Bell Labs Tech. J.,* vol. 4, no. 1, 1999, pp. 163–186.

[13] A. R. Chraplyvy, "High-Capacity Lightwave Transmission Experiments," *Bell Labs Tech. J.,* vol. 4, no. 1, 1999, pp. 230–245.

[14] D. B. Buchholz et al., "Broadband Fiber Access: A Fiber-to-the-Customer Access Architecture," *Bell Labs Tech. J.,* vol. 4, no. 1, 1999, pp. 282–299.

[15] G. C. Wilson et al., "FiberVista: An FTTH or FTTC System Delivering Broadband Data and CATV Services," *Bell Labs Tech. J.,* vol. 4, no. 1, 1999, pp. 300–322.

[16] M. Berger et al., "Pan-European Optical Networking Using Wavelength Division Multiplexing," *IEEE Commun. Mag.,* vol. 35, no. 4, 1997, pp. 82–88.

[17] B. Fabianek, K. Fitchew, S. Myken, and A. Houghton, "Optical Network Research and Development in European Community Programs: From RACE to ACTS," *IEEE Commun. Mag.,* vol. 35, no. 4, 1997, pp. 50–56.

[18] D. Cotter, J. K. Lcek, and D. D. Marcenac. "Ultra-High-Bit-Rate Networking: From the Transcontinental Backbone to the Desktop," *IEEE Commun Mag.,* vol. 35, no. 4, 1997, pp. 90–96.

[19] S. F. Midkiff, "Fiber Optic Backbone Boosts Local-Area Networks, *IEEE Circuits Devices Mag.,* vol. 8, no. 1, 1992, pp. 17–21.

[20] E. Traupman, P. O'Connell, G. Minnis, M. Jadoul, and H. Mario, "The Evolution of the Existing Infrastructure," *IEEE Commun. Mag.,* vol. 37, no. 6, 1999, pp. 134–139.

[21] A. G. Malis, "Reconstructing Transmission Networks Using ATM and DWDM," *IEEE Commun. Mag.,* vol. 37, no. 6, 1999, pp. 140–145.

[22] R. K. Snelling, "Bringing Fiber to the Home," *IEEE Circuits Devices Mag.,* vol. 7, no. 1, 1991, pp. 23–25.

[23] H. Toba and K. Nosu, "Optical Frequency Division Multiplexing Systems: Review of Key Technologies and Applications," *IEICE Trans. Commun.,* vol. E75, no. 4, 1992, pp. 243–255.

[24] O. E. DeLange, "Wide-Band Optical Communication Systems: Part II—Frequency-Division-Multiplexing," *Proc. IEEE,* vol. 58, no. 10, 1970, pp. 1683–1690.

[25] D. K. Hunter et al., "WASPNET: A Wavelength Switched Packet Network," *IEEE Commun. Mag.,* vol. 37, no. 3, 1999, pp. 120–129.

[26] E. Modiano, "WDM-Based Packet Network," *IEEE Commun. Mag.,* vol. 37, no. 3, 1999, pp. 130–135.

[27] H. Kobrinski, R. M. Bulley, M. S. Goodman, M. P. Vecchi, and C. A. Bracket, "Demonstration of High Capacity in the LAMBDANET Architecture: A Multi-Wavelength Optical Network," *Electron. Lett.,* vol. 23, 1987, pp. 303–306.

[28] R. Glance, K. Pollock, C. A. Burrus, B. L. Kasper, G. Eisenstein, and L. W. Stulz, "Densely Spaced WDM Coherent Optical Star Network," *Electron. Lett.,* vol. 23, no. 17, 1987, pp. 875–876.

[29] N. Takato et al., "128-Channel Polarization-Insensitive Frequency-Selection-Switch Using High-Silica Waveguides on Si," *IEEE Photon. Technol. Lett.,* vol. 2, no. 6, 1990, pp. 441–443.

[30] Y-K. M. Lin, D. Spears, and M. Yin, "Fiber-Based Local Access Network Architectures," *IEEE Commun. Mag.,* Oct. 1989, pp. 64–73.

[31] R. A. Linke, "Optical Heterodyne Communications Systems," *IEEE Commun. Mag.,* Oct. 1989, pp. 36–41.

STANDARDS

[1] ANSI/IEEE 812-1984, "Definition of Terms Relating to Fiber Optics," 1984.

[2] Bellcore GR-1377, "SONET OC-192 Transport Systems Generic Criteria," Issue 3, Aug. 1996.

[3] IEC Publication 60825-1, "Safety of Laser Products—Part 1: Equipment Classification, Requirements and User's Guide," 1993.

[4] IEC Publication 60825-2, "Safety of Laser Products—Part 2: Safety of Optical Fibre Communication Systems," 1998.

[5] IEC Publication 61280-2-1, "Fibre Optic Communication Subsystem Basic Test Procedures; Part 2: Test Procedures for Digital Systems; Section 1—Receiver Sensitivity and Overload Measurement," 1998.

[6] IEC Publication 61280-2-2, "Fibre Optic Communication Subsystem Basic Test Procedures; Part 2: Test Procedures for Digital Systems; Section 2—Optical Eye Pattern, Waveform and Extinction Ratio Measurement," 1998.

[7] ITU-T Recommendation G.650, "Definition and Test Methods for the Relevant Parameters of Single-Mode Fibres," 1996.

[8] ITU-T Recommendation G.652, "Characteristics of a Single-Mode Optical Fiber Cable," Apr. 1997.

[9] ITU-T Recommendation G.653, "Characteristics of a Dispersion-Shifted Single-Mode Optical Fiber Cable," Apr. 1997.

[10] ITU-T Recommendation G.655, "Characteristics of a Non-Zero Dispersion-Shifted Single-Mode Optical Fiber Cable," Oct. 1996.

[11] ITU-T Recommendation G.661, "Definition and Test Methods for the Relevant Generic Parameters of Optical Fiber Amplifiers," Nov. 1996.

[12] ITU-T Recommendation G.662, "Generic Characteristics of Optical Fiber Amplifier Devices and Sub-Systems," July 1995.

[13] ITU-T Recommendation G.663, "Application Related Aspects of Optical Fiber Amplifier Devices and Sub-Systems," July 1995.

[14] ITU-T Draft Recommendation G.664, "General Automatic Power Shut-Down Procedure for Optical Transport Systems," Oct. 1998.

[15] ITU-T Recommendation G.671, "Transmission Characteristics of Passive Optical Components," Nov. 1996.

[16] ITU-T Recommendation G.681, "Functional Characteristics of Interoffice and Long-Haul Line Systems Using Optical Amplifiers, Including Optical Multiplexers," June 1986.

[17] ITU-T Draft Recommendation G.691, "Optical Interfaces for Single Channel SDH Systems with Optical Amplifiers, and STM-64 Systems," Oct. 1998.

[18] ITU-T Draft Recommendation G.692, "Optical Interfaces for Multi-Channel Systems with Optical Amplifiers," Oct. 1998.

[19] ITU-T Recommendation G.707, "Network Node Interface for the Synchronous Digital Hierarchy," 1996.

[20] ITU-T Draft Recommendation G.709, "Network Nodc Interface for the Optical Transport Network (OTN)," Oct. 1998.

[21] ITU-T Draft Recommendation G.798, "Characteristics of Optical Transport Networks (OTN) Equipment Functional Blocks," Oct. 1998.

[22] ITU-T Recommendation G.805, "Generic Functional Architecture of Transport Networks," Oct. 1998.

[23] ITU-T Recommendation G.821, "Error Performance of an International Digital Connection Operating at a Bit Rate below the Primary Rate and Forming Part of an Integrated Services Digital Network, Aug. 1996.

[24] ITU-T Recommendation G.826, "Error Performance Parameters and Objectives for International, Constant Bit Rate Digital Paths at or above the Primary Rate," Feb. 1999.

[25] ITU-T Recommendation G.828, "Error Performance Parameters and Objectives for International, Constant Bit Rate Synchronous Digital Paths," Feb. 2000.

[26] ITU-T Draft Recommendation G.871, "Framework for Optical Networking Recommendations," Oct. 1998.

[27] ITU-T Draft Recommendation G.872, "Architecture of Optical Transport Networks," Oct. 1998.

[28] ITU-T Draft Recommendation G.873, "Optical Transport Network Requirements," Oct. 1998.

[29] ITU-T Draft Recommendation G.874, "Management Aspects of the Optical Transport Network Element," Oct. 1998.

[30] ITU-T Draft Recommendation G.875, "Optical Transport Network Management Information Model for the Network Element View," Oct. 1998.

[31] ITU-T Recommendation G.911, "Parameters and Calculation Methodologies for Reliability and Availability of Fibre Optic Systems," 1993.

[32] ITU-T Recommendation G.955, "Digital Line Systems Based on the 1544 kbit/s and the 2048 kbit/s Hierarchy on Optical Fibre Cables," 1993.

[33] ITU-T Recommendation G.957, "Optical Interfaces for Equipments and Systems Relating to the Synchronous Digital Hierarchy," 1995.

[34] ITU-T Recommendation G.958, "Digital Line Systems Based on the Synchronous Digital Hierarchy for Use on Optical Fibre Cables," 1994.

[35] ITU-T Draft Recommendation G.959, "Optical Networking Physical Layer Interfaces," Feb. 1999.

[36] Telcordia GR-253, "Synchronous Optical Network (SONET) Transport Systems: Common Generic Criteria," Issue 2, Dec. 1995.

[37] Telcordia TR-NWT-233, "Digital Cross Connect System," Nov. 1992.

[38] Telcordia TR-NWT-917, "Regenerator," Oct. 1990.

6

TOWARD DWDM FAULT MANAGEMENT AND CURRENT ISSUES

6.1 INTRODUCTION

DWDM is a technology that promises to increase the bandwidth per fiber at incredible levels as the bit rate and the number of wavelengths keep increasing. DWDM systems and networks are engineered to be applicable in long-haul applications, in metropolitan and local area networks, as well as in access networks. Currently, systems with few (6–8) or many (40–160) wavelengths are reality, and at 2.5–40 Gbps per optical channel they transport an amazing aggregate bandwidth up to several Tbps per fiber.

DWDM technology promises long fiber spans (100 km or more) without amplification. The significance of this is clear if, for example, one considers that a SONET repeater may cost thousands of dollars per fiber in addition to maintenance cost. Transmitting without amplification more bandwidth and more wavelengths over longer distances is a news item that certainly does not go unnoticed.

Because of the high aggregate bandwidth and the many innovations that go in a multiwavelength optical network, DWDM networks must have the capability to detect faults (e.g., broken fiber, faulty port unit, inoperable node, malfuntioning components). In addition, they must have the ability to isolate and locate a fault and quickly take a remedial action, either autonomously or via network fault management. The final objective is to offer continuous transmission (service) or service with the minimum disruption possible and with the maximum quality of signal. One of the outstanding issues that network architects have to answer is, when a fault is fixed, does the network return to the previous state quickly or does it continue to remain at that same state until another fault is encountered? This and many other questions can be best addressed if, in addition to standards, software, and management, there is a comprehensive knowledge of the DWDM optical components and their failure mechanisms.

DWDM is a technology that depends heavily on optical components (Figure 6.1), many of which are state of the art. Research continues to innovate and de-

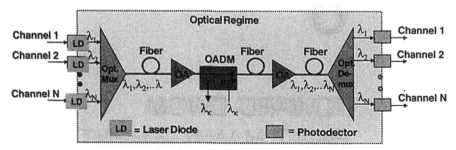

Figure 6.1 A DWDM point-to-point with many of the key optical components.

velop new and better performing optical materials and components, to integrate more than one function in a single component, and to make components more compact and at lower cost. Amplifiers, switches, multiplexers, filters, signal conditioners, transmitter arrays, receiver arrays, and miniature interconnecting devices are among them. In addition, standard transport protocols and network management standards for interoperability are necessary to detect faults and errors in traffic flow, to initiate consequent actions, to correlate defects, and to report failures. The goal is to develop compatible systems conforming to standards and a reliable system and network that assures high-quality signal and service and minimal downtime. If old traditional voice services can demand downtime as short as minutes per year, then how short should the downtime be considering bandwidths of terabits per second?

In communications networks, a defect and an anomaly are clearly defined. Their definition however varies from technology to technology, and a complete discussion on this topic is beyond our scope. Therefore, we encourage the reader to consult the appropriate Fault management document. For example, a defect in ATM may be due to loss of signal (LOS) or to a transmission path alarm indication signal (TP-AIS), whereas in SDH an anomaly may be due to error blocks (EBs) as indicated by the error detection code (EDC) and a fault may be due to a broken fiber. Here, it suffices to say that many faults that affect the optical signal translate into defects. Hence, reliable and fast fault remedial mechanisms translate into defect avoidance, increased traffic availability of the network as well as traffic performance against network link degradations. Figure 6.2 illustrates the case of a dual-ring architecture whereby when a broken fiber is detected the ring automatically reconfigures itself for continuous service.

The following attempts to identify and describe some current issues and areas of intense research and also to summarize the work in this book. Areas not mentioned are not minimized; we merely cannot mention them all.

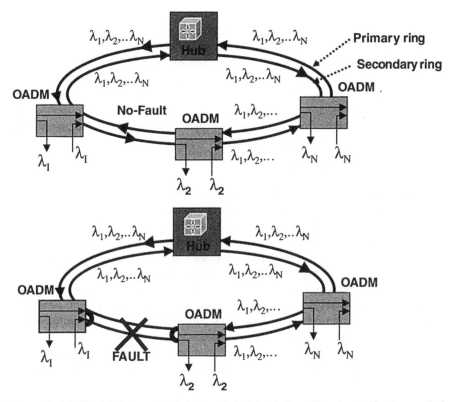

Figure 6.2 A DWDM dual-ring network that is able to detect faults and to u-turn traffic via an optical cross-connect, thus avoiding the faulty link.

6.2   TOWARD FAULT MANAGEMENT

Performance monitoring encompasses all functions and operations that monitor the level or quality of the signal manifested by the rate of errored bits (BER) as well as the time density of errored bits (e.g., errored bit seconds). As already described, the quality of the optical signal in DWDM may be degraded by one or more factors (linear and nonlinear interactions as well as component degradations/failures) as detailed herein. Performance parameters, by and large at the physical layer, are continuously monitored, and any deviations from the accepted value are reported to the system performance manager. Although spurious noise conditions (e.g., bursts of noise) may affect the signal quality and performance sporadically, performance may also be affected persistently by a faulty condition in one or more optical components on the signal path (e.g., filter, amplifier, laser). Such faults then become the object of fault management.

Fault management within a network element (NE) encompasses all these functions and operations that aim at fault detection, fault correlation, fault localization and isolation, service restoration, and fault remedial actions. Service restoration is the ultimate goal, and fault detection is the first step to accomplish that. When a network element detects a failure condition, it generates a fault notification. A fault notification may cause an alarm state. Since a fault may affect the client's service, it is critical that service is restored in real time. This may be accomplished by either restoring service by finding an alternate path or isolating the fault and replacing the faulty circuit with a functional one.

6.2.1 The Network Level

Finding an alternate path is a function at the network level and is typically implemented by executing routing algorithms and communications protocols. In this case, it is implied that the optical network has available bandwidth, reserve protection paths, and supports restoration functions on both the architectural and algorithmic levels. In addition, the path termination endpoints are equipped with fault-detecting mechanisms. These mechanisms have filtering criteria, and reports are sent to the NE fault management system. The latter identifies the fault types, correlates faults, classifies the fault severity level, issues possible alarms, archives the fault attributes, and communicates the results to a network fault management application whose task it is to isolate the fault and trigger consequent remedial actions.

Equipment failure in the upstream direction may affect the transmission signal in the downstream direction, and a single failure may cause many fault notifications. Similarly, a single failure may involve many signal paths (e.g., a fiber cut in DWDM transmission), again each causing a flood of messages. These are fault management issues that need to be addressed so that the network is not flooded with unnecessary messages.

In summary, two types of fault information are of importance, "fault type" and "fault location" (FT&FL). Typically, there has been allocated overhead bandwidth for reporting fault status to all NEs on the "path," "line," and/or "section", if we follow the SONET/SDH nomenclature. In the optical transport network (OTN), more layers are being defined, yet the OTN, like the SONET/SDH, defines a synchronous optical mechanism to transport payload of many clients that are contained in the payload section of an OTN frame. One of the major differences of the OTN frame is a forward error correction (FEC) code that has been included to detect and correct errors. Thus, because of the added FEC, the OTN optical signal becomes more resilient to many optical noise sources. Standards are currently drafted to define the exact meaning, allocation, and function of overhead for FT&FL, which is designed to inform NEs in both upstream and downstream directions.

6.2.2 The NE Level

Replacing a faulty circuit is implimented locally by the NE. In this case, it is implied that the NE has been equipped with protection circuitry to replace the faulty circuit. The NE has fault detection mechanisms with filtering criteria that identify various fault types and issue reports to a NE fault management system. The latter correlates faults, classifies the fault severity level, generates fault notification messages that trigger remedial actions, issues possible alarms, and archives the fault type and location. Here, reports cause the (non-real-time) eventual replacement of the faulty circuit by personnel. As in the previous case, a single failure may involve many signal paths (e.g., a DWDM fiber cut) that may cause a flood of messages to the NE processor.

6.3 CURRENT ISSUES

6.3.1 Optical Supermaterials

Artificial new solid-state optical materials with unusual characteristics are in the experimental stage. Their characteristics are based on extremely high values of the index of refraction, polarization, and switching properties when a varying field is applied. Other artificially induced material properties are based on highly dynamic optical energy absorption and coherent photoluminesence over a wide spectrum range that covers the C- and L-bands or beyond.

In addition, researchers are experimenting with organic compounds that can absorb one wavelength and emit another (for wavelength conversion) or they can absorb a wavelength and emit it back when it is stimulated (optical memory).

6.3.2 Integration

Optical integration will also be the "next step" in the evolution of optical devices. Integration combined with sophisticated packaging will yield devices with complex functionality that could perform optical signal processing with no need to convert the optical signal to electrical. It will not be long when optical devices will follow a similar path evolution as the transistor and the intergrated devices did. A few years ago it was a dream to approach a million transistors in a chip. Today, this dream is past tense and unimpressive.

6.3.3 Lasers and Receivers

Low-cost lasers are important in many applications. Some researchers are even experimenting with organic compounds to create inexpensive high-density plastic lasers and other components.

Development of high-power tunable inexpensive lasers and laser arrays with narrow line width and sufficient optical power for DWDM applications is another activity.

A similar activity is to produce tunable receivers and receiver arrays at low cost. In this venue, some have succeeded in generating hundreds of wavelength channels with a single laser.

6.3.4 Line-Coding Techniques

As the number of wavelengths per fiber increases (reaching 1000 or more), and as the number of bits per second increases (currently 40 Gbps and increasing), the optical signal becomes more vulnerable to errors due to dispersion and other linear and nonlinear phenomena. This increased vulnerability, however, should not compromise in any way the quality of the signal; the signal must be maintained at the acceptable and expected level despite the aggregate bandwidth benefit. This means that signal error countermeasures must be developed to compensate for and correct induced errors on the signal.

Such countermeasures may be based on new line coding techniques that are intersymbol interference (ISI) resistant, on error detection/correction mechanisms that are able to locate and correct errors, or on a combination of both line coding and error correction. A metric of good line coders (for 10 Gbps) is to produce an acceptable eye diagram at the receiver such that the uncertainty of the state (1 or 0) of the received bits is less than 1 bps/Hz. Error rates (as specified in ITU-T standards) may be less than 10^{-12} BER.

6.3.5 Optical Cross-Connect

As the number of wavelengths per fiber increases to numbers exceeding 200 and approaching 1000, 1000 $\times$ 1000, or more optical cross-connect switching fabrics with low insertion loss, nonblocking and fast switching optical systems are a challenge. Today, there is a substantial effort to develop high-density devices with switching matrices based on MEMS technology.

However, research continues to engineer better and faster optical switching methods. Currently, there is research underway to develop ultrafast switching devices based on glasses that contain chalcogenides. Chalcogenide glasses (Ge-Se-Te) have an index of refraction 1000 times higher than SiO_2 glass, an ultrafast response time (they can switch from high nonlinear absorption to low) of less than 1 ps, a low linear loss and a low nonlinear loss β, and a high figure of merit (FOM), on the order of 20.

6.3.6 Optical Add-Drop Multiplexers

Low-cost optical add-drop multiplexers are key components in optical networks. OADM devices allow to drop off and add wavelengths selectively and pass through all other wavelengths. Low-loss and low-cost OADM devices that add/drop groups of wavelengths on a selective basis are another challenge.

The day the fiber will be connected with the desktop computer and multimedia devices is not too far. The bit rate to the home at 64 kbps in the 1960s will be higher than 1.5–2 Mbps in the 2000s (in some cases it may be up to 50 Mbps). These applications will demand extremely low cost and reliable optical devices (transmitters, receivers, and filters).

6.3.7 Optical Memories and Variable Delay Lines

Optical delay lines consist of fiber cut at lengths that, based on travel time of light in the fiber medium, can delay light by a fixed amount of time. This principle is already used in monolithic interferometers. However, compact optical devices that can store a light pulse of as long as it is needed would construct a true optical memory and a controllable delay. Such devices would be used to treat light pulses in a similar manner as electronic pulses and construct optical integrated subsystems with time-division as well as computation properties.

6.3.8 Nonintrusive Optical Monitoring

Nonintrusive optical signal monitoring, although difficult to perform, is very important. The optical signal must be monitored for power, noise, "eye" closure (enough power to be detected by the receiver), wavelength accuracy, and line width. In addition, if a system carries supervisory information, including telemetry, over an optical channel, then this channel needs to be monitored and either be terminated or passed transparently. In general, nonintrusive optical monitoring reduces the amount of optoelectronics, reduces latency, and increases reliability.

6.3.9 DWDM System Dynamic Reconfigurability

System dynamic reconfigurability implies wavelength and bandwidth management as well as fast tunable optical devices (lasers, receivers, filters, and optical cross-connects).

6.3.10 Optical Backplanes

The incoming optical signal at a port is monitored and the optical signal is directly coupled to an optical backplane that routes the signals to another unit of the system, such as an optical cross-connect fabric. Optical backplanes provide a cost-effective and compact solution.

6.3.11 Fault Management Standards

Currently, standards for different layers of the optical network have been adopted, others are in the draft phase, and others in the proposal phase. As DWDM evolves, new standards proposals that address emerging issues on all aspects of DWDM systems, networking, and management are expected. However, fault management means different things to different networks and topologies. Clearly, fault management in a metropolitan application cannot be the same as that in a long-haul transport network. Fault management in low-bit-rate applications (e.g., 622 Mbps cannot be the same with that of a very high bit rate (e.g., 40 Gbps). And fault management cannot be the same in voice and in Internet supporting networks.

Another issue in fault management is self-managed networks (networks that do not require an external operating system to reconfigure the network for network survivability and uninterrupted service). In this case, which topologies are prevalent to self-management? How is network reliability and availability monitored from a centralized location? And along the same lines, there are questions related to scalability and flexibility of the network, as well as to provisioning and to billing.

6.3.12 Network Issues

DWDM technology in optical networks is new ground, and thus many issues not addressed before are emerging. Currently, there is a vast amount of work in progress to resolve these issues. Some examples are as follows:

- Are all nodes in the DWDM network optically transparent or are they opaque?
- If they are transparent, then how do we establish end-to-end (from optical source to destination) wavelength connectivity?
- How do we determine the optimum number of optical components on the end-to-end optical connection (the number of optical components may not be the same from one end to the other) throughout the network?
- How do we rework existing systems and networks to be compatible or interoperable with the new ones?
- How do we perform performance monitoring (PM) in the optical regime?
- What are the rules and the mechanisms for fault detection, fault avoidance, and fault restoration on the optical node level, the optical network level, the fiber level, and the wavelength level?
- What are the rules and the mechanisms for DWDM network survivability?
- How do we configure the system/network (locally versus remotely)?
- How do we implement a supervisory channel (in-band versus out-of-band or over a separate optical channel)?
- How do we assure service reliability, service integrity, and quality of signal as well as quality of service (QoS) in a DWDM network with the same domain and across different domains?
- How do we assure that different network operators observe the same rules?
- What are the mechanisms for optical network management?
- How do we transport over the same DWDM network a variety of services [Internet Protocol (IP), SONET/SDH, asynchronous transfer mode (ATM), Ethernet-type, other]?
- How do we assign or reassign wavelengths across a DWDM optical network in the same domain or across different domains?
- How do we assure security of network and of data?
- As DWDM systems are further deployed and evolve, how do we cope with new emerging issues?

- When a fault is detected in the traffic flow, what is the actual scenario for inserting FDI (forward defect indicator) and AIS (alarm indication signal) to suppress numerous alarms in the downstream of the fault location? Or should there be another mechanism? And, should there be a forward and a backward fault location report? Or, do we need a fault-type indicator and perhaps a fault cause indicator? And should we have an automatic power shutdown?

- What are the advantages of EDC (error detection correction) codes in the optical signal?

- How much can we adopt/modify from the SONET/SDH networks and what do we have to add to the IP? How can we use from existing protocols what perform best and modify the ones that do not? How can we converge to a unified standard that satisfies data, voice, video, and multimedia services?

6.3.13 Opaque Systems

DWDM technology increases the aggregate bandwidth in a fiber, and large systems terminate many fibers. Thus, the aggregate system bandwidth is the sum of the aggregate bandwidth of each fiber. For example, a system with 10 fibers, 40 wavelengths/fiber, and 2.5 Gbps/wavelength has an aggregate bandwidth of 1 Tbps. Presently, an *all-optical* switching system with a capacity of terabits per second is dominated by optical device cost and by ultrafast electronic devices for clock recovery, signal equalization, framing, synchronization, and switching. Thus, currently, systems at such bandwidth levels are by and large electro-optical (opaque), that is, the system itself is electronic and the interfaces and transmission medium is optical.

6.4 ENGINEERING DWDM SYSTEMS: CONCLUSION

To summarize, the design of DWDM systems requires attention to a number of key issues. Not including cost, the following key parameters influence the design of a system and a network (not listed in priority order):

- Nominal center frequencies (wavelengths)
- Channel capacity
- Channel width
- Channel spacing or channel separation
- Channel bit rate and modulation
- Multichannel frequency stabilization
- Channel performance
- Channel dispersion

- Polarizations issues
- Power launched
- Power received
- Optical amplification
- Fiber type used as the transmission medium
- Optical power budget
- Fault detection and fault recovery
- Fault management
- Quality of the signal
- Quality of the service
- Type of services supported
- Service protection and uninterrupted service offering
- Aggregate bandwidth management
- Protocol used to transport supported services
- Protocol for network management
- Network reliability
- Network protection and survivability
- Network scalability and flexibility
- System and network reconfigurability
- Supervisory channels and protocols
- Wavelength management
- Interoperability
- Interdomain compatibility
- Supervisory channel(s); in-band and out-of-band

REFERENCES

[1] S. V. Kartalopoulos, *Introduction to DWDM Technology: Data in a Rainbow,* IEEE Press, New York, 2000.

[2] S. V. Kartalopoulos, *Understanding SONET/SDH and ATM: Communications Networks for the Next Millennium,* IEEE Press, New York, 1999.

[3] S. V. Kartalopoulos, "Aspects in Fault Detectability," *Proceedings of ACM'2000,* London, Nov. 14–16, 2000, to be published.

[4] R. Ramaswami and K. N. Sivarajan, *Optical Networks,* Morgan Kaufmann, San Francisco, CA, 1998.

[5] B. Mukherjee, *Optical Communication Networks,* McGraw-Hill, New York, 1997.

[6] I. P. Kaminow, Ed., and T. L. Koch, Ed., *Optical Fiber Communications IIIA and Optical Fiber Communications IIIB,* Academic, New York, 1997.

[7] E. Traupman, P. O'Connell, G. Minnis, M. Jadoul, and H. Mario, "The Evolution of the Existing Infrastructure," *IEEE Commun. Mag.,* vol. 37, no. 6, 1999, pp. 134–139.

[8] A. G. Malis, "Reconstructing Transmission Networks Using ATM and DWDM," *IEEE Commun. Mag.,* vol. 37, no. 6, 1999, pp. 140–145.

[9] T-H Wu, *Fiber Network Service Survivability,* Artech House, Boston, 1992.

[10] L. Boivin, M. C. Nuss, W. H. Knox, and J. B. Stark, "206-Channel Chirped-Pulse Wavelength-Division Multiplexed Transmitter," *Electron. Lett.,* vol. 33, no. 10, 1997, pp. 827–828.

[11] J. M. Simmons et al., "Optical Crossconnects of Reduced Complexity for WDM Networks with Bidirectional Symmetry," *IEEE Photon. Technol. Lett.,* vol. 10, no. 6, 1998, pp. 819–821.

[12] E. A. De Souza et al., "Wavelength-Division Multiplexing with Femtosecond Pulses," *Opt. Lett.,* vol. 20, no. 10, 1995, pp. 1166–1168.

[13] S. V. Kartalopoulos, "An Associative RAM-Based CAM and Its Application to Broad-Band Communications Systems," *IEEE Trans. Neural Networks,* vol. 9, no. 5, 1998, pp. 1036–1041.

[14] S. V. Kartalopoulos, "Ultra-Fast Pattern Recognition in Broadband Communications Systems," *ISPACS'98 Conference Proceedings,* Melbourne, Australia, Nov. 1998.

[15] S. V. Kartalopoulos, "The λ-Bus in Ultra-fast DWDM Systems," to be published.

[16] S. V. Kartalopoulos, "Synchronization Techniques Ultra-Fast DWDM Systems: The λ-bus," to be published.

[17] S. V. Kartalopoulos, "Add-Drop with Ultra-fast DWDM/λ-Bus," to be published.

[18] S. V. Kartalopoulos, "Increasing Bandwidth Capacity in DWDM/λ-Bus Systems," to be published.

[19] S. V. Kartalopoulos, "Cryptographic Techniques with Ultra-fast DWDM/λ-Bus Systems," to be published.

[20] C. A. Brackett, "Dense Wavelength Division Multiplexing Networks: Principles and Applications," *IEEE JSAC,* vol. 8, no. 6, 1990, pp. 948–964.

[21] H. Yoshimura, K-I. Sato, and N. Takachio, "Future Photonic Transport Networks Based on WDM Technologies," *IEEE Commun. Mag.,* vol. 37, no. 2, 1999, pp. 74–81.

[22] L. H. Sahasrabuddhe and B. Mukherjee, "Light-Trees: Optical Multicasting for Improved Performance in Wavelength-Routed Networks," *IEEE Commun. Mag.,* vol. 37, no. 2, 1999, pp. 67–73.

[23] M. A. Marsan, A. Bianco, E. Leonardi, A. Morabito, and F. Neri, "All-Optical WDM Multi-Rings with Differentiated QoS," *IEEE Commun. Mag.,* vol. 37, no. 2, 1999, pp. 58–66.

[24] Y. Pan, C. Qiao, and Y. Yang, "Optical Multistage Interconnection Networks: New Challenges and Approaches," *IEEE Commun. Mag.,* vol. 37, no. 2, 1999, pp. 50–56.

[25] K. Sato, *Advances in Transport Network Technologies—Photonic Networks, ATM and SDH,* Artech House, Boston, 1996.

[26] N. Takachio and S. Ohteru, "Scale of WDM Transport Network Using Different Types of Fibers," *IEEE JSAC,* vol. 16, no. 7, 1998, pp. 1320–1326.

[27] B. Mukhergie, *Optical Communications Networks,* McGraw-Hill, New York, 1997.

[28] P. E. Green, Jr., *Fiber Optic Networks,* Prentice-Hall, Englewood Cliffs, NJ, 1993.

[29] M. A. Marsan et al., "Daisy: A Scalable All-Optical Packet Network with Multi-Fiber Ring Topology," *Computer Networks ISDN Syst.,* vol. 30, 1998, pp. 1065–1082.

[30] I. Gidon and Y. Ofek, "MetaRing—a Full-Duplex Ring with Fairness and Spatial Reuse," *IEEE Trans. Commun.,* vol. 41, no. 1, 1993, pp. 110–120.

[31] S. Ohteru and K. Inoue, "Optical Time Division Multiplexer Utilizing Modulation Signal Supplied to Optical Modulation as a Reference," *IEEE Photon,* vol. 8, no. 9, 1996, pp. 1181–1183.

[32] J. R. Freer, *Computer Communications and Networks,* IEEE Press, New York, 1996.

[33] R. Handel and M. N. Huber, *Integrated Broadband Network,* Addison-Wesley, Reading, MA, 1991.

[34] R. D. Gitlin, J. F. Hayes, and S. B. Weinstein, *Data Communications Principles,* Plenum, New York, 1992.

[35] S. V. Kartalopoulos, "A Manhattan Fiber Distributed Data Interface Architecture," in *Proceedings of IEEE Globecom'90,* San Diego, Dec. 2–5, 1990.

[36] S. V. Kartalopoulos, "Disaster Avoidance in the Manhattan Fiber Distributed Data Interface Network," in *Proceedings of IEEE Globecom'93,* Houston, TX, Dec. 2, 1993.

[37] S. V. Kartalopoulos, "A Plateau of Performance?" *IEEE Commun. Mag.,* Sept. 1992, pp. 13–14.

[38] A. E. Willner, "Mining the Optical Bandwidth for a Terabit per Second," *IEEE Spectrum,* Apr. 1997, pp. 32–41.

[39] S. V. Kartalopoulos, *Understanding Neural Networks and Fuzzy Logic,* IEEE Press, New York, 1995.

[40] Members of the Technical Staff, *Transmission Systems for Communications,* Bell Telephone Laboratories, New York, 1982.

[41] J. Nellist, *Understanding Telecommunications and Lightwave Systems,* IEEE Press, New York, 1996.

[42] W. Y. Zhou and Y. Wu, "COFDM: An Overview," *IEEE Trans. Broadcasting,* vol. 41, no. 1, 1995, pp. 1–8.

STANDARDS

[1] ITU-T Recommendation G.702, "Digital Hierarchy Bit Rates," 1988.

[2] ITU-T Draft Recommendation G.691, "Optical Interfaces for Single Channel SDH Systems with Optical Amplifiers, and STM-64 Systems," Oct. 1998.

[3] ITU-T Draft Recommendation G.692, "Optical Interfaces for Multi-Channel Systems with Optical Amplifiers," Oct. 1998.

[4] ITU-T Recommendation G.707, "Network Node Interface for the Synchronous Digital Hierarchy," 1996.

[5] ITU-T Draft Recommendation G.709, "Network Node Interface for the Optical Transport Network (OTN)," Oct. 1998.

[6] ITU-T Draft Recommendation G.798, "Characteristics of Optical Transport Networks (OTN) Equipment Functional Blocks," Oct. 1998.

[7] ITU-T Recommendation G.805, "Generic Functional Architecture of Transport Networks," Oct. 1998.

[8] ITU-T Draft Recommendation G.871, "Framework for Optical Networking Recommendations," Oct. 1998.

[9] ITU-T Draft Recommendation G.872, "Architecture of Optical Transport Networks," Oct. 1998.

[10] ITU-T Draft Recommendation G.873, "Optical Transport Network Requirements," Oct. 1998.

[11] ITU-T Draft Recommendation G.874, "Management Aspects of the Optical Transport Network Element," Oct. 1998.

[12] ITU-T Draft Recommendation G.875, "Optical Transport Network Management Information Model for the Network Element View," Oct. 1998.

[13] ITU-T Recommendation G.911, "Parameters and Calculation Methodologies for Reliability and Availability of Fibre Optic Systems," 1993.

[14] ITU-T Recommendation G.957, "Optical Interfaces for Equipments and Systems Relating to the Synchronous Digital Hierarchy," 1995.

[15] ITU-T Recommendation G.958, "Digital Line Systems Based on the Synchronous Digital Hierarchy for Use on Optical Fibre Cables," 1994.

[16] ITU-T Draft Recommendation G.959, "Optical Networking Physical Layer Interfaces," Feb. 1999.

[17] Telcordia GR-253, "Synchronous Optical Network (SONET) Transport Systems: Common Generic Criteria," Issue 2, Dec. 1995.

ACRONYMS

10BaseT	10 Mbps over twisted pair
100BaseT	100 Mbps over twisted pair
1000BaseT	1000 Mbps over twisted pair
2FSK	Two-level frequency shift keying
3R	Reshaping, retiming, and reamplifying
8B/10B	Eight-bit to 10-bit coding
AA	Adaptive antenna
AAL	ATM adaptation layer
ABM	ATM buffer management
ABR	Available bit rate
AC	Authentication counter; alternating current
ACD	Automatic call distribution system
ACSE	Association control service element
ACTS	Advanced Communications Technology and Services
ADBF	Advanced digital beam forming
ADC	Analog-to-digital conversion
ADM	Add-drop multiplexer
ADPCM	Adaptive differential pulse code modulation
ADSL	Asymmetric digital subscriber line
ADTS	Automated digital terminal equipment system
AFI	Authority format identifier
AFNOR	Association Francaise de Normalisation
AFR	Absolute frequency reference

AGC	Automatic gain control
AH	Applications header
AIS	Alarm indication signal; aka blue alarm
AIU	Access interface unit
AIX	Advanced interactive executive
Al	Aluminum
ALTS	Alternative Local Transmission System
AM	Administration module; amplitude modulation
AMAC	American Market Awareness and Education Committee
AMF	Asian Multimedia Forum
AMI	Alternate mark inversion
AMPS	Advanced Mobile Phone Service
AN	Access node
ANSI	American National Standards Institute
AON	All Optical Network
AOTF	Acousto-optic tunable filter
AP	Access point; adjunct processor
APC	Adaptive predictive coding
APD	Avalanche photodetector; Access procedure-D channel
APDU	Application protocol data unit; Authentic protocol data unit
APON	ATM-based broadband PON
APS	Automatic protection switching
AR	Antireflecting (coating)
ARM	Access Resource Management
ARPA	Advanced Research Project Agency
ARQ	Automatic repeat request
As	Arsenic
AS&C	Alarm, surveillance, and control
ASBC	Adaptive subband coding
ASE	Amplified spontaneous emission; application service element
ASK	Amplitude shift keying
ASP	Adjunct service point
ATM	Asynchronous transfer mode
ATU	ADSL transceiver unit
ATU-C	ATU central office
ATU-R	ATU remote terminal
AU	Administrative unit

AU-AIS	Administrative unit AIS
AUG	Administrative unit group
AU-LOP	Administrative unit loss of pointer
AU-N	Administrative unit level N
AU-NDF	Administrative unit new data flag
AU-PJE	Administrative unit pointer justification event
AWG	Array waveguide grating
AWGN	Additive white gaussian noise
BAS	Broadband access signaling
BB	Broadband
BBE	Background block error
BBER	Background block error ratio
BCC	Block check character; blocked-calls-cleared
BCCH	Broadcast control channel
BCD	Binary-coded decimal; Blocked-calls-delayed
BCF	Burst coordination function
BDCS	Broadband Digital Cross-Connect System
BDI	Backward defect indication
BDMA	Band division multiple access
BECN	Backward explicit congestion notification
BER	Bit error rate; basic encoding rules
BFSK	Binary FSK
BICI	Broadband Inter-Carrier Interface
BIM	Byte-interleaved multiplexer
BIP	Bit-interleaved parity
BIP-8	Bit-interleaved parity 8 field
BISDN	Broadband Integrated Services Digital Network
BITS	Building Integrated Timing System
BLER	Block error rate
BLSR	Bidirectional line-switched ring
BnZS	Bipolar n-zero substitution, $n=3, 6, 8$
BPF	Bandpass-filter
bps	Bits per second
BPSK	Binary PSK
BRI	Basic rate interface
BS	Burst second

BSHR	Bidirectional shelf healing ring
BSHR/2	Two-fiber bidirectional shelf healing ring
BSHR/4	Four-fiber bidirectional shelf healing ring
BSI	British Standards Institution
BSS	Broadband Switching System; basic service set
BTS	Bit Transport System
BV	Bipolar violation
BW	Bandwidth
C-n	Container-level n, $n=11$, 12, 2, 3, 4
CAC	Connection admission control
CAD	Computer-aided design
CAGR	Cumulative average growth rate
CAM	Content addressable memory; computer-aided manufacture
CAP	Carrierless amplitude phase; competitive access provider
CARIN	Center for Applied Research in Information Networking
CAS	Channel-associated signaling
CBMS	Computer-Based Message System
CBR	Constant bit rate
CC	Composite clock
CCAF	Call Control Agent System
CCC	Clear channel capability
CCF	Call control function
CCI	Compliant client interface
CCITT	Consultative Committee International Telegraph and Telephone (renamed ITU)
CCM	Cross-connect multiplexing
CCR	Current cell rate
CCSN	Common Channel Signaling Network
CD	Chromatic dispersion
CDC	Chromatic dispersion coefficient
CDMA	Code division multiple access
CDPD	Cellular digital packet data
CDR	Call detail record
CDV	Cell delay variation
CDVT	Cell delay variation tolerance
CEI	Connection endpoint identifier
CEIGU	Channel estimation and interference generation unit

CELP	Code excited linear prediction
CEPT-n	Conference of European Posts and Telecommunications-level n (see E1)
CER	Cell error rate
CES	Circuit Emulation Service
CEU	Committed end user
CF	Conventional (single-mode) fiber
CFP	Contention-free period
CI	Congestion indicator
CICS	Customer information control subsystem
CIM	Common information model
CIR	Committed information rate
CIT	Craft interface terminal
CIU	Channel interface unit
CLASS	Custom Local Area Signaling Services
CLEC	Competitive local exchange carrier
CLIP	Channel loading independent performance
CLLI	Common language location identifier
CLNP	Connectionless Network Layer Protocol
CLP	Cell loss priority
CLR	Cell loss rate
CLTP	Connectionless Transport Layer Protocol
CM	Communications module; connection management
CMI	Coded mark inversion
CMIP	Common Management Information Protocol
CMISE	Common Management Information Service Element
CMIS/P	Common Management Information Service/Protocol
CMOS	Complementary metal–oxide–semiconductor
CNM	Customer network management
CNTRL	Control
CO	Central office
CODEC	Coder-decoder
COFDM	Coded orthogonal frequency-division multiplexing
COMSIC	Coherent multistage interference canceller
COP	Connection Oriented Protocol
CORBA	Common object request broker architecture
CoS	Class of service
COT	Central office terminal

COTS	Commercial off-the-shelf technology/equipment
CP	Customer premises; control point; connection point; communications processor
CPCS	Common part of convergence sublayer
CPDU	Computer protocol data unit
CPE	Customer premises equipment
CPFSK	Continuous-phase FSK
CPN	Calling party's number; Customer Premises Network
CPRING	Client protection ring
CPWDM	Chirped-pulse WDM
CRBS	Cell Relay Bearer Service
CRC	Cyclic redundancy check
CRM	Cell rate margin
CRS	Cell Relay Service
CS	Convergence sublayer
CSA	Carrier serving area
CSES	Consecutive severely errored seconds
CSI	Convergence sublayer indicator
CSMD/CD	Carrier sense multiple access/collision detection
CSMF	Conventional single-mode fiber
CS-PDU	Convergence sublayer-PDU
CSU	Channel service unit
CT-2	Cordless telephone version 2
CTD	Cell transfer delay
CTI	Computer-Telephony Integration
CU	Channel unit
CV	Coding violation
CVSDM	Continuous variable slope delta modulation
CW	Continuous wave
CWDM	Coarse-wavelength division multiplexer
DA	Dispersion accommodation
DACS	Digital Access and Cross-Connect System
DAMA	Demand assignment multiple access
DARPA	Defense Advanced Research Projects Agency
dB	Decibel
DBF	Digital beam forming
dBm	Decibel with 1 mW reference level

DBR	Distributed Bragg reflector
DC	Direct current
DCB	Digital channel bank
DCC	Data country code; data communication channel; digital clear channel
DCE	Data circuit-terminating equipment
DCF	Dispersion compensation fiber; distributed coordination function
DCME	Digital compression multiplex equipment
DCN	Data Communications Network
DCOM	Distributed component object model
DCS	Digital Cross-Connect System
DDCMP	Digital Data Communications Message Protocol
DDD	Direct distance dialing
DDE	Dynamic data exchange
DDS	Digital Data Service
DECT	Digital European Cordless Telecommunications System
DES	Data encryption standard
DFB	Distributed feedback
DFCF	Dispersion-flattened compensated fiber
DFF	Dispersion-flattened fiber
DFI	Domain format identifier
DGD	Differential group delay
DH	Dual homing
DHCP	Dynamic Host Configuration Protocol
DIN	Deutsches Institut fuer Normung EV
DIP	Dual in-line package
DIU	Digital interface unit
DLC	Digital loop carrier
DLCI	Data link connection identifier
DLL	Delay-lock tracking group
DMT	Discrete multitone modulation
DNHR	Dynamic nonhierarchical routing
DOA	Direction of arrival
DOP	Degree of polarization
DP	Diverse protection
DPA	Dynamic packet assignment
DPBX	Digital PBX
DPCM	Differential pulse code modulation

DPDU	Data link PDU
DPE	Distributed processing environment
DPSK	Differential PSK
DQDB	Distributed queue dual bus
DR	Digital radio; dynamical routing
DRI	Dual-ring interface
DSAP	Destination service access point
DSBSC	Double-sideband suppressed carrier
DS-CDMA	Direct-sequence CDMA
DSCF	Dispersion-shift compensated fiber; dispersion-slope compensated fiber
DSF	Dispersion-shifted fiber
DSI	Digital speech interpolation
DSL	Digital subscriber line
DSLAM	Digital subscriber line access multiplexer
DS-n	Digital signal level n, $n=0$, 1, 2, 3
DSP	Domain-specific part; digital signal processor
DS-SMF	Dispersion-shifted single-mode fiber
DSSS	Direct-sequence spread spectrum
DST	Dispersion-supported transmission
DSU	Data service unit
DSX-n	Digital signal cross-connect point for DS-n signals
DTE	Data terminal equipment
DTF	Dielectric thin film
DTMF	Dual-tone multifrequency
DTS	Digital Termination Service
DWDM	Dense wavelength-division multiplexing
DXC	Digital cross-connect
DXC 4/4	DXC with a maximum VC-4 interface and VC-4 cross-connecting fabric
DXI	Data exchange interface
E1	Wideband digital facility at 2.048 Mbps, also called CEPT-1
E3	Broadband digital facility at 34.368 Mbps, also called CEPT-3
E4	Broadband digital facility at 139.264 Mbps, also called CEPT-4
EA	Address extension; electroabsorption
EB	Error block

EBC	Errored block count
EBCDIC	Extended binary-coded decimal interchange code
EC	Echo canceller; embedded channel
ECC	Embedded communication channel
ECMA	European Association for Standardizing Information and Communication Systems
ECSA	Exchange Carriers Standards Association
EDC	Error detection code
EDCC	Error detection and correction code
EDFA	Erbium-doped fiber amplifier
EDI	Electronic data interchange
EFI	Errored frame indicator
EFS	Error-free second
EIA/TIA	Electronics Industry Association/Telecommunications Industry Association
EIM	External interface module
EIR	Excess information rate; Equipment Identity Register
ELAN	Emulated LAN
EM	Element manager; electromagnetic
EMA	Expectation Maximization Algorithm
EMAC	European, Middle East, and Africa Market Awareness and Education Committee
EMC	Electromagnetic compatibility
EMI	Electromagnetic interference
EML	Element management layer
EMS	Element Management System
E-n	European signal level n ($n=1, 2, 3, 4$)
E/O	Electrical to optical
EOC	Embedded operations channel
EPD	Early packet discard
EPM	Enhanced performance monitoring
EQTV	Extended-quality TV
ER	Electronic regenerator
ES	Error second
ESCON	Enterprise Systems connectivity
ESF	Extended superframe format
ESR	Errored seconds ratio

ET	Extra traffic
ETRI	Electronics and Telecommunications Research Institute
ETSI	European Telecommunications Standardization Institute
EX	Extinction ratio
EXC	Electronic cross-connect
F	Fluoride
FACCH	Fast associated control channel
FACH	Forward access channel
FAS	Frame alignment signal; fiber array switch
FBG	Fiber Bragg grating
FBS	Fiber bundle switch
FC	Functional component
FCC	Federal Communications Commission
FCS	Frame check sequence
FD	Frame discard
FDD	Frequency-division duplex
FDDI	Fiber-distributed data interface
FDI	Feeder distribution interface; forward defect indicator
FDM	Frequency-division multiplexing
FDMA	Frequency-division multiple access
FEBE	Far-end block error
FEC	Forward error correction
FECN	Froward explicit congestion notification
FEP	Front-end processor
FER	Frame error rate
FERF	Far-end receive failure
FET	Field effect transistor
FEXT	Far-end cross-talk
FFT	Fast Fourier transform
FFTS	Fiber feeder transport system
FH	Frequency hopping
FHSS	Frequency-hopped spread spectrum
FITL	Fiber in the loop
FM	Frequency modulation
FOA	First office application; fiber-optic amplifier
FOM	Figure of merit

FOT	Fiber-optic terminal
FOTS	Fiber Optic Transmission System
FP	Fabry-Perot
FPI	Fabry-Perot interferometer
FPM	Four-photon mixing
FPS	Fast packet switching
FR	Frame relay
FRAD	Frame relay assembler/disassembler
FRAMES	Future Radio Wideband Multiple Access System
FRF	Frame-Relay Forum
FRI	Frame relay interface
FRS	Frame relay service
FRSP	Frame relay service provider
FSAN	Full Services Access Network
FSBS	Free-space beam steering
FSK	Frequency shift keying
FSR	Free spectral range
FT	Fixed transmitter
FTAM	File transfer and access method
FTP	File Transfer Protocol
FTTB	Fiber to the building
FTTC	Fiber to the curb
FTTCab	Fiber to the cabinet
FTTD	Fiber to the desk
FTTH	Fiber to the home
FTTO	Fiber to the office
FTTT	Fiber to the town
FUNI	Frame user network interface
FWA	Fixed wireless access
FWHM	Full width at half-maximum
FWM	Four-wave mixing
FX	Foreign exchange
FXC	Fiber cross-connect
Ga	Gallium
Gbps	Gigabits per second, equals 1000 Mbps
GCRA	Generic Cell Rate Algorithm

GD	Group delay
GDMO	Guidelines for the definition of managed objects
GEF	Gain equalization filter
GFC	Generic flow control
GHz	Gigahertz (10^9 Hz)
GI	Group identification
GII	Global Information Infrastructure
GMPCS	Global Mobile Personal Communications Satellite
GNE	Gateway network element
GoS	Grade of service
GPS	Global Positioning System
GRIN	Graded-index fiber
GSC	Global Standards Collaboration
GSM	Global System for Mobile Communications
GUI	Graphical user interface
HCDS	High Capacity Digital Services
HCS	Hierarchical cell structure
HDB3	High-density bipolar 3 zeroes substitution
HDBn	High-density bipolar n zeroes allowed
HDLC	High-level data link control
HDSL	High-bit-rate digital subscriber line
HDT	Host digital terminal
HDTV	High-definition TV
HDX	Half-duplex
HEC	Header error control
HFC	Hybrid fiber coax
HIPERLAN	High Performance Radio Local Area Network
HIPPI	High-performance parallel interface
HLR	Home Location Register
HPF	High-pass filter
HP-PLM	High-order payload label mismatch
HP-RDI	High-order RDI
HP-REI	High-order REI
HP-TIM	High-order TIM
HP-UNEQ	High-order path unequipped
HTML	Hyper-Text Markup Language
HTR	Hard to reach

HTU	HDSL terminal unit
HVC	High-order virtual container
IANA	Internet Assigned Number Authority
IBSS	Independent basic service set
IC	Integrated circuit; interference canceller
ICC	Interstate Commerce Commission
ICCF	Interchange Carrier Compatibility Forum
ICD	International code designator
ICI	Intercarrier interference; Intercarrier interface
ICIP	Inter-Carrier Interface Protocol
ICR	Initial cell rate
ICSR	Incremental cost-to-survivability ratio
ID	Identifier
IDI	Initial-domain identifier
IDL	Interface Definition Language
IDLC	Integrated digital loop carrier
IDP	Initial-domain part
IDSL	ISDN DSL
IEC	Interstate Electrotechnical Commission
IEEE	Institute of Electrical and Electronics Engineers
IETF	Internet Engineering Task Force
IFFT	Inverse fast Fourier transforms
IL	Insertion loss
ILEC	Incumbent local exchange carrier
ILMI	Interim local management interface
IM	Intensity modulation; inverse multiplexer; intelligent multiplexer
IMA	Inverse multiplexing over ATM
IMAC	Isochronous medium-access controller
IM/DD	Intensity modulation with direct detection
IMS	Information Management System
IMT-2000	International Mobile Telecommunications-2000
In	Indium
IN	Intelligent Network
IOF	Interoffice framework
IP	Internet Protocol; intelligent peripheral
IPgn	Internet Protocol next generation
IPNNI	Integrated PNNI

IPv6	Internet Protocol version 6
IPX	Inter-Network Packet Exchange
IR	Infrared
IrDA	Infrared Data Association
ISA	Industry standard architecture
ISDN	Integrated Services Digital Network
ISI	Intersymbol interference
ISM	Intelligent or integrated synchronous multiplexer
ISO	International Standards Organization
ISOC	Internet Society
ISP	Internet service provider
ITSP	Internet telephony service provider
ITU	International Telecommunications Union
ITU-D	ITU development sector
ITU-R	ITU radiocommunications sector
ITU-T	ITU telecommunications standardization sector
IW	Interworking
IWF	Interworking function
IWU	Interworking unit
IXC	Interexchange carrier
JIDM	Joint Inter-domain Management Group
JIT	Jitter transfer function
JMAPI	Java Management API
JTC1	Joint Technical Committee 1 (ISO/IEC)
kbps	Kilobits per second, equals 1000 bps
KTN	Kernel Transport Network
LA	Line amplifier
LAC	Link access control
LAN	Local area network
LANE	Local area network emulation
LAPD	Link Access Protocol for the D Channel
LAPF	Link Access Protocol for Frame Relay
Laser	Light amplification by stimulated emission or radiation
LATA	Local-access and transport area
LB	Loop back

LBO	Line build-out
LC	Link connection
LCM	Least common multiplier
LCN	Logical channel number
LCV	Line coding violations
LD	Laser diode; long distance
LEC	Local exchange carrier
LED	Light-emitting diode
LENO	Line equipment number originating
LENT	Line equipment number terminating
LEOS	Low Earth Orbit Satellite
LES	Line errored seconds
LF	Line feed; low frequency
LiNbO$_3$	Lithium niobate
LLC	Logical link control
LO	Low order
LOF	Loss of frame
LOH	Line overhead
LOM	Loss of multiframe
LOP	Loss of pointer
LO-PLM	Low-order PLM
LO-RDI	Low-order RDI
LO-REI	Low-order REI
LO-RFI	Low-order remote failure indication
LOS	Loss of signal; loss of synchronization
LO-TIM	Low-order TIM
LO-UNEQ	Low-order UNEQ
LPC	Linear prediction coding
LPF	Low-pass filter
LRC	Longitudinal redundancy check
LSB	Least significant bit
LSES	Line severed errored seconds
LSO	Local serving office
LSS	Loss of sequence synchronization
LSSU	Link status signaling unit
LTE	Line termination equipment
LU	Logical unit
LVC	Low-order virtual container

LWPF   low water peak factor

M1   Level 1 multiplexer
M2   Level 2 multiplexer
M11c   Two DS1 multiplexer for T1c rates
M12   Level 1-to-2 multiplexer
M13   Level 1-to-3 multiplexer
M23   Level 2-to-3 multiplexer
MAC   Media-specific access control
MAF   Management application function
MAI   Multiple-access interference
MAN   Metropolitan area network
Mbps   Megabits per second, equals 1000 kbps
MBS   Maximum burst rate
MCF   Message communications function
MCN   Management Communications Network
MCR   Maximum cell rate
MCS   Multicast server
MCTD   Mean cell transfer delay
MCVD   Modified chemical vapor deposition
MD   Mediation device
MDF   Main distribution frame
MEMS   Microelectromechanical system
MEOS   Medium Earth Orbit Satellite
MF   Mediation function; matching filter
MFL   Multifrequency laser
MHz   Megahertz, 10^6 Hz
MI   Management information; Michelson interferometer; modulation instability
MIB   Management information base
MII   Ministry of the (China) Information Industry
MLM   Multilongitudinal mode
MLSE   Maximum-likelihood sequence estimator
MMDS   Multichannel Multipoint Distribution Service
MO   Managed object
MONET   Multiwavelength optical networking
MOS   Mechanical-optical switches

MoU	Memorandum of understanding
MPEG	Motion Picture Experts Group
MPI	Main path interface; multipath interface
MPI-R	main path interface at the receiver
MPI-S	main path interface at the transmitter
MPN	Mode partition noise
MPOA	Mutli-Protocol over ATM
MQW	Multiple quantum well
MS-AIS	Multiplex section AIS
MSB	Most significant bit
MSC	Mobile switching center
MSDSL	Multirate SDSL
msec	Milliseconds
MS-FERF	Multiplex section FERF
MSK	Minimum shift keying
MSN	Manhattan street network
MSO	Multiple-service operator
MSOH	Multiplexer section overhead
MSP	Multiplex section protection
MS-RDI	Multiplex section remote defect indication
MS-REI	Multiplex section remote error indication
MSRN	Mobile station roaming number
MSS	Mobile Satellite Service
MS-SPRING	Multiplex section–shared protection ring
MSTE	Multiplex section terminating equipment, also called LTE
MSU	Message signal unit
MTBF	Mean time between failure
MTIE	Maximum time interval error
MTJ	Maximum tolerable jitter
MTP	Message transfer part
MTSO	Mobile telephone switching office
MUD	Multiuser detection
MUMPS	Multiuser MEMS process
μsec	Microseconds
MUX	Multiplexer
MVL	Multiple virtual lines
mW	Milliwatts

MWM	Multiwavelength meter
MZI	Mach-Zehnder interferometer
NANP	North American numbering plan
NAP	Network access provider
NASA	National Aeronautics and Space Administration
NAU	Network addressable unit
NC	Network connection
NC&M	Network control and management
NCI	Noncompliant client interface
NCP	Network control point; network control program
Nd	Neodymium
NDF	New data flag
NDIS	Network driver interface specification
NE	Network element
NEBS	Network Equipment Building System
NEF	Network element function
NEXT	Near-end cross-talk
NF	Noise figure
NGI	Next-generation Internet
NHRP	Next Hop Resolution Protocol
NIC	Network interface card
NID	Network interface device; network information database
NIST	National Institute for Standards and Testing
NIU	Network interface unit
NLSS	Nonlocally switched special
nm	Nanometer
NML	Network management layer
NMS	Network Management System
NNI	Network-to-network interface
NOB	Network operator byte
NPC	Network parameter control
NPDU	Network Protocol data unit
NPI	Null pointer indication
NRL	Naval Research Laboratory
NRM	Network resource management
NRZ	Nonreturn to zero
ns	Nanosecond

NSA	National Security Agency
NSN	Network service node
NSP	Network service provider
NT	Network termination
NTSC	National Television Standards Committee
NTU	Network termination unit
NZDF	Nonzero dispersion (shifted) fiber
NZSMF	Nonzero dispersion single-mode fiber

OA	Optical amplifier
OADM	Optical ADM
OAM	Operations, administration, and management
OAMP	OAM and Provisioning Services
OAR	Optically amplified receiver
OAS	Optical amplifier section
OAT	Optically amplified transmitter
OC	Optical carrier
OCDM	Optical code-division multiplexing
OCh	Optical channel
OC-n	Optical carrier level n ($n=1$, 3, 12, 48, 192)
ODL	Optical data link
ODMA	Open distributed management architecture
ODP	Optical diverse protection; open distributed processing
ODU	Optical demultiplex unit
O-E	Optical-to-electrical conversion
OEIC	Opto-electronic integrated circuit
OEM	Original equipment manufacturer
OFA	Optical fiber amplifier
OFD	Optical frequency discriminator
OFDM	Optical frequency-division multiplexing; orthogonal frequency-division multiplexing
OFS	Optical Fiber System
OH	Overhead; hydroxile
OLA	Optical limiting amplifier
OLC	Optical loop carrier
OLE	Object linking and embedding
OLS	Optical Line System
OLTM	Optical line-terminating multiplexer

OLTS	Optical loss test set
OMA	Object management architecture
OMAP	Operations, maintenance, and administration part
OMG	Object Management Group
OMS	Optical Multiplex System; optical multiplex section
OMU	Optical multiplex unit
ONTC	Optical Networks Technology Consortium
ONU	Optical network unit
OOF	Out of frame
OOK	On-off keying
OOS	Out of synchronization
OPLDS	Optical Power Loss Detection System
OPLL	Optical phase-locked loop
OPM	Optical protection module
OPS	Optical protection switch
ORL	Optical return loss
OS	Operating system
OSA	Optical spectrum analyzer
OSC	Optical supervisory channel
OSF	Operating system function
OSI	Open system interconnect
OSI-RM	Open system interconnect reference model
OSNR	Optical signal-to-noise ratio
OSPF	Open shortest path first
OSS	Operator Service System
OTDM	Optical time-division multiplexing
OTDR	Optical time-domain reflectometer
OTE	Optical terminating equipment
OTS	Optical transmission section
OTU	Optical transponder unit
OUI	Organization unit identifier
OVSE	Orthogonal variable spreading factor
OXC	Optical cross-connect
P	Phosphorus
PACS	Personal Access Communications System
PAD	Packet assembler and disassembler

PAM	Pulse amplitude modulation
PBS	Polarization beamsplitter
PBX	Private Branch Exchange
PC	Payload container; protection channel; personal computer
PCH	Prechirp
PCM	Pulse code modulation
PCR	Peak cell rate
PCS	Personal Communication Services
PD	Photodiode; propagation delay
PDC	Passive dispersion compensation
PDFA	Praseodymium doped fiber amplifier
PDH	Plesiochronous digital hierarchy
PDL	Polarization-dependent loss
PDN	Packet Data Network; Passive Distribution System
PDU	Protocol data unit
PE	Payload envelope
PEP	Product evolution planning
PHB	Polarization hole burning
PHS	Personal Handy-phone System
PHY	Physical layer
PIC	Photonic integrated circuit
PIM	Personal information manager
PIN	Positive-intrinsic-negative (photodiode)
PJ	Pointer justification
PJC	Pointer justification count
PKS	Public key cryptosystem
PLC	Planar lightwave circuit
PLCP	Physical Layer Convergence Protocol
PLL	Phase-locked loop
PM	Performance monitoring
PMD	Polarization mode dispersion; physical medium dependent
PMMA	Polymethyl methacrylate
PMO	Present method of operation
PN	Pseudo-random numerical sequence
PNNI	Private NNI
POH	Path overhead
PON	Passive Optical Network

POP	Point of presence
POTS	Plain Old Telephone Service
PP	Pointer processing
ppm	Parts per million
PPP	Point-to-Point Protocol
PPS	Path protection switching
PRBS	Pseudorandom binary sequence
PRC	Primary reference clock
PRI	Primary rate interface
PRK	Phase reversal keying
PRS	Primary reference source
PRSG	Pseudorandom sequence generator
PS	Protection switching; phase shift
PSC	Public Service Commission; protection switching count
PSD	Protection switching duration; power spectral density
PSK	Phase shift keying
PSTN	Public Switched Telephone Network
PTE	Path-terminating equipment
PTI	Payload type identification
PTO	Public telephone operator
ptp	Peak to peak
PTT	Postal Telephone and Telegraph ministries
PUC	Path user channel
PVC	Permanent virtual circuit
PVP	Permanent virtual path
Q3	TMN interface
QAM	Quadrature amplitude modulation
QDU	Quantizing distortion unit
QoS	Quality of service; quality of signal
QPSK	Quadrature PSK; quartenary PSK; quadriphase PSK
RAC	Remote access concentrator
RACE	Research of Advanced Communications Technologies in Europe
RADSL	Rate adaptive DSL
RBOC	Regional Bell Operating Company
RDF	Rate decrease factor

RDI	Remote defect indicator, formerly FERF; also called yellow alarm
REI	Remote error indicator
RF	Radio frequency
RFI	Remote failure indication; radio-frequency interference
RIF	Rate interface factor
RISC	Reduced instruction set computer
RLP	Radio Link Protocol
RM	Resource management
RMS	Root-mean-square
ROM	Read-only memory
ROSE	Remote operation service element
RRM	Radio Resource Management
RSM	Remote switch module
RSOH	Regenerator section overhead
RSTE	Regenerator section terminating equipment
RS-TIM	RS trace identifier mismatch
RSU	Remote switch unit
RSVP	Resource Reservation Setup Protocol
RT	Remote terminal
RTS	Return to send; residual time stamp
RTT	Round-trip time; Radio Transmission Technology
RTU	Remote termination unit
RZ	Return to zero
SAAL	Signaling AAL
SACCH	Slow associated control channel
SAGE	Space-alternating generalized EMA
SAI	Serving area interface
SAP	Service access point
SAR	Segmentation and reassembly
SAR-PDU	SAR payload data unit
SAT	Supervisory audio tone
SATATM	Satellite ATM
SAW	Surface acoustic wave (filter)
SBS	Stimulated Brillouin scattering
SCAM	Supplemental channel assignment message
SCC	Specialized common carrier

SCF	Service control function
SCO	Serving central office
SCP	Service control point
SCPC	Single channel per carrier
SCR	Sustainable cell rate
SCV	Section coding violation
SD	Signal degrade
SDCU	Satellite delay compensation unit
SDH	Synchronous Digital Hierarchy
SDLC	Synchronous Data Link Control Protocol
SDM	Space-division multiplexing
SDSL	Symmetric DSL
SDU	Service data unit
SEC	SDH equipment clock
SECB	Severely errored cell block
SEED	Self electro-optic effect device
SEFS	Severely errored frame seconds
SEPI	Severely errored period intensity
SES	Severely errored second
SESR	Severely errored seconds ratio
SF	Signal fail; superframe; spreading factor; single frequency
SFL	Single-frequency laser
SH	Single homing
SHR	Self-healing ring
SI	Step index
SIFS	Short interframe space
$\Sigma\Delta$PCM	Sigma-delta PCM
SIM	Subscriber identity module
SIP	SMDS Interface Protocol; series in-line package
SIR	Signal-to-interference ratio
SL	Submarine lightwave
SLA	Service level agreement
SLC	Synchronous line carrier
SLM	Synchronous line multiplexer
SM	Switching module
SMASE	System management application service element
SMDS	Switched Multi-megabit Digital Services
SMF	Single-mode fiber; Service Management Function

SML	Service management layer
SMN	SONET Management Network; SDH Management Network
SMS	SDH Management Subnetwork
SMSR	Side-mode suppression ratio
SN	Sequence number; service node
SNA	Systems Network Architecture
SNAP	Subnet Access Protocol
SNC	Subnetwork connection
SNC/Ne	Subnetwork connection protection/intrusive end-to-end monitoring
SNC/Ns	Subnetwork connection protection/nonintrusive sublayer monitoring
SNCP	Subnetwork connection protection
SNI	Service node interface; subscriber-to-network interface; SMDS network interface
SNICF	Subnetwork independent convergence function
SNMP	Simple Network Management Protocol
SNMS	Subnetwork Management System
SNP	Sequence number protection
SNR	Signal-to-noise ratio
SOA	Semiconductor optical amplifier
SOH	Section overhead
SOHO	Small office/home office
SONET	Synchronous Optical Network
SP	Switching point
SPDU	Session Protocol data unit
SPE	Synchronous payload envelope
SPM	Self-phase modulation
SPRING	Shared protection ring
S-PVC	Soft PVC
S/R	Signal-to-noise ratio
SR	Software radio; symbol rate
SRF	Specialized resource function
SRS	Stimulated Raman scattering
SRTS	Synchronous residual time stamp
SS7	Signaling system 7
SSAP	Source service access point; session service access point (ISO)
SSB	Single sideband
SS-CDMA	Spread-spectrum CDMA

SSCF	Service-specific coordination function
SSCOP	Service-Specific Connection Oriented Protocol
SSCP	System services control point
SSCS	Service-specific CS
SSL	Secure socket layer
SSM	Synchronization status message
SSMF	Standard single-mode fiber
SSR	Side-mode suppression ratio
STB	Set top box
STDM	Statistical TDM
STE	Section-terminating equipment; switching terminal exchange
STM-n	Synchronous transport module level n ($n=1$, 4, 16, 64)
STP	Shielded twisted pair; signal transfer point
STS	Synchronous transport signal; space-time-space switch
SVC	Switched virtual circuit
SWAP	Shared Wireless Access Protocol
SWC	Service wire center

T1	Digital carrier facility used to transmit a DS1 signal at 1.544 Mbps
T3	Digital carrier facility used to transmit a DS3 signal at 45 Mbps
TA	Terminal adapter
TASI	Time assignment speech interpolation
Tbps	Terabits per second, equals 1000 Gbps
TCAM	Telecommunications access method
TCAP	Transaction capabilities part
TCM	Tandem connection monitoring; trellis code modulation
TCP	Transmission Control Protocol; trail connection point
TCP/IP	Transmission Control Protocol/Internet Protocol
TDD	Time-division duplex
TDE	Time-domain extinction
TDEV	Time deviation
TDM	Time-division multiplexing
TDMA	Time-division multiple access
TE	Terminal equipment; transverse electric
TEC	Thermoelectric cooler
Te-EDFA	Tellurium-EDFA
TEI	Terminal endpoint identifier

tFWM	Temporal FWM
TH	Transport header
THz	Terahertz, equals 1000 Ghz
TIA	Telecommunications Industry Association
TIM	Trace identifier mismatch
TINA	Telecommunications Information Networking Architecture Consortium
TM	Traffic management; terminal multiplexer; transverse magnetic
TMM	Transmission monitoring machine
TMN	Telecommunications Management Network
TOF	Tunable optical filter
TOH	Transport overhead (SOH + LOH)
ToS	Type of service
TP	Twisted pair; Transport Layer Protocol
TP-AIS	Transmission path alarm indication signal
TPC	Transmit power control
T&R	Tip and ring
TS	Time Stamp; time slot
TSB	Telecommunications Systems Bulletin
TSE	Test sequence error
TSG	Timing signal generator
TSI	Time slot interchanger
TST	Time-space-time switch
TT	Trail termination
TTA	Telecommunications Technology Association
TU	Tributary unit
TU-AIS	Tributary unit AIS TU-LOP; tributary unit LOP
TUC	Total user cell number
TUG-n	Tributary unit group n, $n = 2, 3$
TU-LOM	Tributary unit loss of multiframe
TU-n	Tributary unit level n, $n = 11, 12, 2, 3$
TU-NDF	Tributary unit NDF
UAS	Unavailable second
UAT	Unavailable time
UAWG	Universal ADSL Working Group
UBR	Unspecified bit rate

UCAID	University Corporation for Advanced Internet Development
UDC	Universal digital channel
UDP	User Datagram Protocol
UHF	Ultrahigh frequency
UI	Unit interval
UME	UNI management entity
UMTS	Universal Mobile Telecommunications System
UNEQ	Unequipped
UNI	User-to-network interface
UPC	Usage parameter control
UPSR	Unidirectional path switch ring
URL	Uniform resource locator
USART	Universal synchronous/asynchronous receiver transmitter
USF	(dispersion) Unshifted single-mode fiber
USHR	Unidirectional shelf-healing ring
USTIA	United States Telecommunications Industry Association
UTOPIA	Universal test and operations interface for ATM
UTP	Unshielded twisted pair
UUID	Universal unique ID
UWBA	Ultra-wide-band amplifier
VBR	Variable bit rate
VC	Virtual channel
VCC	VC connection
VCCG	Voltage-controlled code generator
VCI	Virtual circuit identifier
VC-n	Virtual container level n, $n=2, 3, 4, 11, 12$
VC-n-Mc	Virtual container level n, M concatenated virtual containers
VCSEL	Vertical-cavity surface-emitting laser
VDSL	Very-high-bit-rate DSL
VF	Voice frequency
VGL	Voice grade line
VHF	Very-high frequency
VLAN	Virtual LAN
VLF	Very-low frequency
VLSI	Very-large-scale integration
VOA	Variable optical attenuator
VOD	Video on demand

VoIP	Voice over IP
VP	Virtual path
VPC	VP connection
VPI	Virtual path identifier
VPN	Virtual Private Network
VR	Virtual radio
VT	Virtual tributary
VTAM	Virtual telecommunications access method
VTOA	Voice Telephone over ATM
WADM	Wavelength add-drop multiplexer
WAN	Wide area network
WATM	Wireless ATM
WATS	Wide Area Telephone Service
WB-DCS	Wideband Digital Cross-Connect System
WBEM	Web-Based Enterprise Management
W-CDMA	Wideband DS-CDMA
W-DCS	Wideband Digital Cross-Connect System
WDM	Wavelength-division multiplexing
WER	Word error rate
WGR	Waveguide grating router
WIPO	World Intellectual Property Organization
WIS	Wavelength independent switch
WIXC	Wavelength interchanging cross-connect
WLAN	Wireless LAN
WMSA	Weighted multislot averaging
WPON	WDM PON
WSC	Wavelength selective coupler
WSS	Wavelength selective switch
WSXC	Wavelength selective cross-connect
WTR	Wait to restore
X.25	Packet switching international standard
xDSL	Any-DSL
XOR	Exclusive OR logic function
XPM	Cross-phase modulation
YIG	Yttrium-iron-garnet
ZBTSI	Zero-byte TSI

INDEX

ABOUT THE AUTHOR

Stamatios V. Kartalopoulos is currently with the Transport & Networking Architecture Department of the Advanced Optical Networking Organization of Lucent Technologies, Bell Labs Innovation (formerly known as AT&T). Dr. Kartalopoulos holds a B.Sc. in physics, a graduate diploma in electronics, and a M.Sc. and Ph.D. in electrical engineering.

Dr. Kartalopoulos' responsibilities have been in SONET/SDH and ATM architectures, ATM payload mapping over SONET/SDH, controller architectures, high-efficiency scalable protocols, digital cross-connects, switching systems, local area networks, transmission and access systems, complex VLSIs, neural networks and fuzzy logic, and microprocessor-based real-time architectures. In addition to his technical expertise in systems and networks, he has led and managed focus teams in technical marketing and customer service with responsibility in both Europe and the United States. His most recent activities have been in the definition of Optical

Transport Network Overhead (OTN-OH), in the definition of DWDM Fault Detectability of Optical Platforms, in the survivability of Optical Networks, and in the definition of the supervisory channel protocol for WDM metro applications.

Dr. Kartalopoulos has published three books, *Introduction to DWDM Technology: Data in a Rainbow* (IEEE Press, 2000), *Understanding SONET/SDH and ATM: Communications Networks for the Next Millennium* (IEEE Press, 1999), and *Understanding Neural Networks and Fuzzy Logic: Basic Concepts and Applications* (IEEE Press, 1996). This book, *Fault Detectability in DWDM: Toward Higher Signal Quality & System Reliability* is his second in the series of DWDM technology books. Dr. Kartalopoulos has also contributed chapters to other books and he has been a guest editor of *IEEE Communications Magazine,* as well as editor in chief of a technical in-house publication. Also, he has published more than 40 scientific articles.

Dr. Kartalopoulos has been awarded 10 patents, and has submitted seven applications in optical communications. Having been an IEEE Distinguished Lecturer, he has lectured on DWDM technology, on SONET/SDH, on ATM, on Neural Networks, and on Fuzzy Logic at international conferences of IEEE and SPIE as well as in academic forums. He is a member of IEEE (the editor in chief of the IEEE Press Board, past vice president, and committee chair), of Sigma Xi, and of Etta Kappa Nu. He has received the President Award, the Award of Excellence, and numerous certificates of appreciation.

Printed and bound by CPI Group (UK) Ltd, Croydon, CR0 4YY

27/10/2024

14580334-0002